"...As my Father hath sent me, even so send I you."
John 20:21

Do you desire to follow more closely in the Lord's footsteps? Turn to these inspiring books by Robert E. Coleman:

The Master Plan of Evangelism This thorough examination of the Gospel accounts reveals the objective of Christ's ministry and His strategy for carrying it out.

The Master Plan of Discipleship Dr. Coleman studies the Book of Acts to help you and your church be more effective in carrying out the Great Commission today.

The Mind of the Master This unique book focuses on Christ's inner thought life as revealed in Scripture, especially the Gospel narratives. Learn how to make Jesus' thoughts your thoughts so you can continue the ministry He bequeathed to you.

"Dr. Robert Coleman, one of the most important voices for evangelism in America, has pointed the way to reach past the cynicism of modern secular man. The church has the message and the means to effect this change. Dr. Coleman has given us the method."

Jess Moody, Pastor
First Baptist Church of Van Nuys, California

BY Robert E. Coleman

Established by the Word
Introducing the Prayer Cell
Life in the Living Word
The Master Plan of Evangelism
The Spirit and the Word
Dry Bones Can Live Again
One Divine Moment (Editor)
Written in Blood
Evangelism in Perspective
The Mind of the Master
They Meet the Master
Songs of Heaven
Growing in the Word
The New Covenant
The Heartbeat of Evangelism
Evangelism on the Cutting Edge (Editor)
The Master Plan of Discipleship
The Spark That Ignites
Nothing to Do but to Save Souls
The Great Commission Life-Style

The Great Commission Lifestyle

Conforming Your Life to Kingdom Priorities

Robert E. Coleman

Fleming H. Revell
A DIVISION OF
Baker Book House
Grand Rapids, Michigan

Library of Congress Cataloging-in-Publication Data

Coleman, Robert Emerson.
    The great commission life-style / Robert E. Coleman.
      p.   cm.
    ISBN 0-8007-5450-6
    1. Great Commission (Bible).   I. Title.
BV2074.C64   1992
266—dc20   92-9487
                                      CIP

Copyright © 1992 by Robert E. Coleman
Published by Fleming H. Revell,
A division of Baker Book House
P.O. Box 6287, Grand Rapids, MI 49516-6287
Printed in the United States of America

With thanksgiving for their
prayers and ministry of discipleship,
this book is dedicated to
Lyell Rader, Lyle Dorsett, Gene Warr, and Wayne Watts,
beloved in the bonds of the Great Commission

Contents

"All authority in heaven and on earth has been given to me. Therefore go and make disciples of all nations, baptizing them in the name of the Father and of the Son and of the Holy Spirit, and teaching them to obey everything I have commanded you. And surely I am with you always, to the very end of the age."

Matt. 28:18–20

Preface

Confusion in the Church

A college freshman was wearing a lapel button that had printed on it the letters *BAIK*. When asked what the letters meant, he said, "It means, 'Boy am I confused.' "

"But don't you know," someone reminded him, "confused is not spelled with a *K?*"

"Man," he exclaimed, "you don't know how confused I am!"

The young man's predicament is not unlike that of many people today concerning Christ's commission to disciple all nations. Few subjects, I suspect, are connected with more misunderstanding, if not disbelief.

Some people see the command as directing a few aspiring saints to vocational service in the church. Others think of it as a special call to cross-cultural overseas ministry. To a host of persons, the obligation comes down to little more than giving financial support to missionaries. There are those, of course, who frankly admit that they have no idea what it means. Little wonder that the mission of the church remains unfinished.

From Every Nation

However interpreted, no serious student of Scripture can question God's plan to raise up a people for His praise—a people gathered from every kindred and tribe and language of the earth.

This was His design in the beginning, when He made man and woman in His image and charged them to "be fruitful and multiply, and fill the earth" with His glory (Gen. 1:28 NAS; cf. Ps. 86:9; Is. 43:21; Rev. 4:11). Though the sin of our forebears necessarily brought havoc and death upon the human race, it did not change the divine will. Even when the wickedness of mankind so invokes the wrath of God that He cannot bear their folly anymore, as with the generation of Noah and the arrogant society building the tower of Babel, He will not be defeated in His creative purpose (Gen. 6:1—9:1; 11:9).

God's determination to make a people in His likeness comes beautifully into focus in the call of Abraham to leave the degradation of sin in Ur in the Chaldees, and go to a new land of promise. " 'I will make you into a great nation,' " the patriarch was told. ". . . And all peoples on earth will be blessed through you" (Gen. 12:1–3; cf. 15:1–6; 18:18; 22:18). His posterity was to become ". . . as numerous as the stars in the sky and as countless as the sand on the seashore" (Heb. 11:12; cf. Gen. 15:5); they would spread out " 'like the dust of the earth . . . to the west and to the east, to the north and to the south . . .' " (Gen. 28:14; cf. 13:14–17; 15:1–6; 17:1–7; 18:18, 19; 22:17, 18).

What was revealed to Abraham is repeated again and again to his descendants (Gen. 26:4; 28:4; Ex. 32:13; etc.). Furthermore, his seed is to become God's means of bringing "salvation to the ends of the earth" (Is. 49:6; cf. 42:6). By their holy life-styles "many peoples and powerful nations" would come to see the superior nature of their God and "seek the Lord Almighty" (Zech. 8:22, 23; cf. Is 55:4, 5; Jer. 10:7).

Tragically, however, the chosen people seldom fulfill their

role in world evangelization. More often than not they succumb to the sins of the pagans about them and have neither a witness nor a sense of mission to their neighbors. Jonah's reluctance to go and preach to Nineveh, notwithstanding the command of God, typified in a personal way the normal disposition of Israel (Jonah 1:1—4:11).[1]

Still there were occasions when the vision of God's universal family broke through their parochial self-centeredness, as when Solomon prayed that " 'all the peoples of the earth' " might know and fear the Name of Israel's God (1 Kings 8:43, 60; 2 Chr. 6:33). The Psalmists also spoke of declaring the glory of the Lord to all nations (1 Chr. 16:24; Ps. 97:6; 99:3–5). There were instances, too, when the prophets envisioned a day when all the ends of the earth would turn to God and be saved (Is. 45:22; cf. 66:19), and "the earth will be filled with the knowledge of the glory of the Lord, as the waters cover the sea" (Hab. 2:14).

Coming of the Messiah

This future reign of blessedness was associated with the promised Messiah, to whom the Kingdom "belongs and the obedience of the nations is his" (Gen. 49:10). Through Him evil will be destroyed, justice exalted, righteousness established, and "of the increase of his government and peace there will be no end . . ." (Is. 9:7). These prophecies pointed to the end of history and the return of the triumphant King, "one like a son of man, coming with the clouds of heaven" to reign over His people (Dan. 7:13). He will be "given authority, glory and sovereign power; all peoples, na-

---

1. That Jonah would be called to preach a message of deliverance to this benighted people evidences God's desire to save the nations of the earth. In this instance, gratefully, the reluctant messenger did finally obey the call, and a marvelous revival ensued.

tions and men of every language" will worship Him; and He will receive a Kingdom "that will never be destroyed" (Dan. 7:14). ". . . His rule will extend from sea to sea, and from the River to the ends of the earth" (Zech. 9:10).

Jesus ministered in the joy of this promise. He lived anticipating that day when the redeemed of the nations "will come from the east and the west, and will take their places at the feast with Abraham, Isaac, and Jacob in the kingdom of heaven" (Matt. 8:11). The gathering of His people at the throne of God was in His thinking every time He referred to Himself as the Son of Man (e.g., Matt. 9:6; 12:8; 13:37; 17:12; Mark 2:10; 8:31; Luke 7:34; 19:10; John 3:13; 6:27),[2] just as it throbbed in His heart when He spoke of the Kingdom (e.g., Mark 1:15; Luke 4:43; 8:1; 9:2; 16:16).[3] Recall, as an example, the last supper with His disciples, when He gave the cup to them, saying, " 'I will not drink of this fruit of the vine from now on until that day when I drink it anew with you in my Father's kingdom' " (Matt. 26:29; cf. Mark 14:25). Visions of that destined reunion filled His mind with glory; it flooded His soul even as He prayed on the eve of Calvary (John 17:5, 24).

He realized, of course, that before the nations could bow before Him, He would have to reconcile mankind to God through the sacrificial offering of Himself and the good news of His finished work made known to the ends of the earth.

---

2. The title relates to the conquering King of heaven who will receive the everlasting Kingdom (Dan. 7:13–28). Altogether there are eighty-two occurrences of this description in the Gospels, more than any other self-designation recorded on the lips of Jesus. A concise description of this term, with bibliographic references, will be found in my study *The Mind of the Master* (Old Tappan, N. J.: Fleming H. Revell Co., 1977), 104–107.

3. In proclaiming the truth, Jesus lifted up a theme that runs through the Bible—God reigns over His people. The Kingdom is present in Christ; we enter the Kingdom now when we are born of His Spirit; but its consummation will not come until the King of glory returns to reign over His people. For more information, *see* ibid., 107–110.

In its ultimate realization, then, the coming of the Kingdom awaited the evangelization of the world. Only after the gospel has been preached in all the world as a witness can the end come to which history is moving (Matt. 24:14). It is not difficult to understand why Jesus gave such force to the Great Commission before ascending into the heavens to assume His place at the right hand of the Majesty on high.

Commissioning the Church

All four of the evangelists record the glorified Lord charging His disciples with the task, though each states it from his own unique perspective.[4] John stresses the missionary nature of the commission. Meeting with His disciples on the day of His resurrection, after giving them His peace, Jesus says, " '. . . As the Father has sent me, I am sending you' " (John 20:21). His words echo an earlier concern; when interceding for His dis-

---

4. Treatments of the Great Commission are as varied as they are plentiful. One of the popular biblical expositions is David M. Howard's little volume, *The Great Commission for Today* (Downers Grove, Ill.: InterVarsity Press, 1976). A more recent study by William L. Banks, *In Search of the Great Commission* (Chicago: Moody Press, 1991), gives special attention to the text. John Robson's book *The Resurrection Gospel* (Edinburgh: Olphant Anderson & Ferrier, 1908), belonging to a previous generation, provides one of the most beautiful renderings of the various accounts. Other widely read works are G. Campbell Morgan's *The Missionary Manifesto* (Grand Rapids, Mich.: Baker Book House, 1970, first published 1909) and Samuel M. Zwermer's *Into All the World: The Great Commission—A Vindication and Interpretation* (Grand Rapids, Mich.: Zondervan, 1943). A host of eminent church leaders' and missiologists' writings, all of which in some way treat Christ's world mandate, could be added to the list, including the works of David Hesselgrave, Herbert Kane, J. Christie Wilson, John R. Mott, Henry Boer, Max Warren, Ralph Winter, Stephen Neill, Peter Beyerhaus, Donald McGavran, Michael Pocock, Harold Lindsell, George Peters, James W. Reapsome, John Gration, J. T. Seamonds, Paul Hiebert, Leslie Newbigin, David Barrett, Peter Wagner, A. T. Pierson, H. Wilbert Norton, Paul McKaughan, David J. Bosch, Mortimer Arias, to mention only a few. New Testament commentaries, of course, can be consulted for insight to particular passages of Scripture that bear upon the subject.

ciples, He prayed, "As you sent me into the world, I have sent
them into the world" (John 17:18). The similarity between our
Lord's controlling sense of mission and that of His disciples
cannot be mistaken. Just as He was sent by the Father to carry
out God's purposes—a work now accomplished[5]—so those
who believe on Him receive apostleship and are sent forth in
His name.[6]

It is well to observe, too, the incarnational dimension of
the mission. Christ had to renounce His own rights and take
the form of servant when He was sent into the world. In the
same way, His disciples become an embodiment of the message they bear and live in the world as the Lord has set an
example. Making this witness possible, John concludes the
commission with Christ's promise of the Holy Spirit (John
20:22).

This emphasis also comes through in Luke's rendering of
the commission in the attention to the saving word and empowered witnessing through the Spirit. Having dispelled the
disciples' fear with physical proof of His resurrection, Jesus
explained that what had happened to Him was simply the
fulfillment of Scripture (Luke 24:36–45). " 'This is what is
written: The Christ will suffer and rise from the dead on the

---

5. Though the words for "send" in John 20:21 are different (*apostello* used here of
Christ and in John 17:18 of both Christ and His disciples, means "sent on an official
mission," whereas *pempo*, used here of the disciples, means "sent with purpose"),
little can be gained by making a significant distinction between the terms. However,
the contrast in the tenses of the verbs is worth attention. When "sent" is used in
reference to Christ's mission, the verb is in the perfect tense, which in the Greek
language designates a completed task that has continuing effects. But when "sent"
is used in reference to the disciples, the verb is in the present tense, meaning an
action in progress. A paraphrase might read: "As God the Father has delegated me to
take a human form to do His work on earth, and I have finished what He sent me to
do; now you who know the results of that mission are my sent ones to the world."
6. That the assignment applies to a larger group than the original disciples of Jesus
seems evident from Luke 24:33, probably a parallel passage to John 20:19–23, where
persons other than the eleven are said to be present when the commission was given.

third day, and repentance and forgiveness of sins will be preached in his name to all nations, beginning at Jerusalem. You are witnesses of these things. I am going to send you what my Father has promised; but stay in the city until you have been clothed with power from on high' " (Luke 24:46–49). The Acts record brought out much the same teaching on the Spirit: " 'You will receive power,' " Jesus said, " 'when the Holy Spirit comes on you; and you will be my witnesses in Jerusalem, and in all Judea and Samaria, and to the ends of the earth' " (Acts 1:8).[7]

Witnessing means "to bear testimony to what is known personally to be true." "That . . . which we have heard, which we have seen with our eyes, which we have looked at and our hands have touched," John said, "this we proclaim . . ." (1 John 1:1; cf. Acts 1:22; 5:32; 10:39; 13:31; 1 Pet. 5:1; 2 Pet. 1:16). It includes more than talking, though what we believe should find expression in our speech. Witnessing incarnates the reality of the message so that "it is impossible to separate the meaning of the witness from the content of the witness borne by that person."[8]

Mark puts Christ's accent on the necessity of taking initiative and verbally proclaiming the gospel: " 'Go into all the world and preach the good news to all creation,' " (Mark 16:15). Then, stressing what is at stake in the message,

---

7. Whether or not the commission reported in Acts took place at a later date than that recorded in the Gospel is not clear, but it makes no difference as to the message. The Acts of the Apostles, it should be noted, constitutes the second volume of the Gospel of Luke. The first volume describes ". . . all that Jesus began to do and to teach until the day he was taken up to heaven," whereas Acts chronicles what He continues to do in His church (Acts 1:1; cf. Luke 1:1–4). Luke's record of His witnessing commission, with its emphasis on the Spirit's power, constituted the last utterance of Jesus before He returned to the Father.

8. Darrell L. Guder, *Be My Witnesses* (Grand Rapids, Mich.: Wm. B. Eerdmans, 1985), 41. For a summary description of the term as used in Scripture, *see* H. Strathmann, "Martus," *Theological Dictionary of the New Testament*, ed. Gerhard Kittel, vol. 4 (Grand Rapids, Mich.: Wm. B. Eerdmans, 1972), 475.

Jesus adds: " 'Whoever believes and is baptized will be saved, but whoever does not believe will be condemned' " (Mark 16:16). He mentions, too, that demonstrations of the Spirit's power will accompany those who believe (Mark 16:17, 18).[9]

Prominence is given to proclaiming the redeeming work of the crucified and risen Savior. The verb "preach" is an imperative, expressing an urgent command to herald the message of the one who sends. In this case, it is Christ who tells the messenger what to say, and he or she speaks with His authority.[10]

It should be understood that the preaching described here, as throughout the New Testament, is not limited to formal public delivery associated with a pulpit ministry.[11] The manner and style of speaking the gospel depends upon the situation. What matters is that the unequivocal truth gets to every creature. In this task every believer, wherever sent, is a herald of Christ.

---

9. Some ancient manuscripts do not include Mark 16:9–20 in the Gospel account. However, evidence for the exclusion is not conclusive, and I see no compelling reason to reject the authenticity of the canonical text. *See* R. H. Lightfoot, *The Gospel Message of St. Mark* (Oxford: Clarendon, 1958), 80–97; R. C. H. Lenski, *The Interpretation of St. Mark's Gospel* (Minneapolis: Augsburg, 1964) 750–774.

10. A herald, like the courier of a king, does not create the message proclaimed; the herald only delivers the king's command. In the commission passage of Luke 24:47, where the message is "preached" in Christ's name, the same word is used, but in an aorist infinitive form, which conveys the idea of pointed preaching that is ongoing.

11. In addition to the word *kerusso*, translated "preach" in this commission, Gerhard Friedrich lists thirty-three other words for oral proclamation used in the New Testament. Words that mean "say" or "speak" occur far more often, though we may commonly use them in reference to preaching. "Even if we disregard the other terms, and restrict ourselves to preach in translation of [this word family]," Dr. Friedrich says, "the word is not a strict equivalent of what the New Testament means by [the term]." It "does not mean the delivery of a learned and edifying or hortatory discourse in well chosen words and pleasant voice. It is the declaration of an event." *Theological Dictionary of the New Testament*, ed. Gerhard Kittel, vol. 3 (Grand Rapids, Mich.: Wm. B. Eerdmans, 1965), 703.

The Comprehensive Mandate

The Matthew record of the commission in some degree embraces the thrust of the other three. It begins with the declaration of Christ, "All authority in heaven and on earth has been given to me" (Matt. 28:18). What He asserts here, of course, is implied in the authoritative way disciples are sent forth as well as in the message given them to preach. Jesus is Lord, able to do whatever He wills, and before Him every knee must bow.

This being true, "Therefore," He says to His followers, "go and make disciples of all nations, baptizing them in the name of the Father and of the Son and of the Holy Spirit, and teaching them to obey everything I have commanded you" (Matt. 28:19, 20). The word "go" picks up Mark's emphasis as well as John's concern for the mission of Christ. "Baptizing," the mark of identification with Jesus, incorporates the task of preaching the gospel and witnessing to its power, brought out by Mark and Luke. "Teaching" also is part of the communication process, especially in the building up of believers.

Encompassing all these efforts is discipling. Not only does it involve the other components of ministry—sending, going, preaching, witnessing, baptizing, teaching, and receiving the Spirit[12]—but it directs every activity to the desired end,

---

12. For a concise summary of these mandate words (with the exception of *sending*) showing the Greek verbs or derivatives, the number of usages of the terms, and other immediate cognates in the Greek New Testament and related by nouns and their usage, *see* "Christ's Great Commission Analyzed into Two Minicommissions and Seven Mandates," eds. David B. Barrett and Todd M. Johnson, *AD 2000 Global Monitor*, no. 1 (November 1990), 3. This comprehensive diagram is reprinted in *Mission Frontiers*, 12, no. 12 (December 1990), 39. The more complete review of these words will be found in David Barrett's *Evangelize! A Historical Survey of the Concept* (Birmingham, Ala.: New Hope Press, 1987), in which he traces the big six words associated with "evangelize" in the New Testament. In his work, *World Class Cities and World Evangelization* (Birmingham, Ala.: New Hope Press, 1986), he argues for two major levels of the Great Commission mandate—evangelizing and discipling.

namely, to "make disciples" of Christ—men and women who not only believe the gospel but also continue to follow in the way of Jesus.

The universal scope of this task again is specified in the objective of reaching "all nations." The words do not refer to geographic boundaries, but rather to all peoples of the earth. In the other commissions, Luke's version speaks of "all nations, beginning at Jerusalem" (Luke 24:47), then amplifies it to "all Judea and Samaria, and to the ends of the earth" (Acts 1:8). John relates the mission to the "world" (John 17:18; cf. 20:21); whereas Mark extends it to "all creation," to the whole domain of mankind (Mark 16:15). Clearly God's purpose is to reach every human being with the gospel (1 Tim. 2:4; 2 Pet. 3:9). There is no distinction between home missions and foreign missions: It is all world evangelism.

Stressing that we are laborers together with Christ, the record of Matthew concludes with the promise, " 'And surely I am with you always, to the very end of the age' " (Matt. 28:20). Christ's assurance of His abiding presence, elsewhere attributed to the ministry of the Holy Spirit, brings the commission into a wonderful experience of the reigning Lord. What more need be said? When He is with us, all things are possible.

Plan of This Study

Using the most comprehensive text of the Great Commission—Matthew—as an outline, this study unfolds around the

---

He argues that the church cannot be reaching every person and discipling at the same time, with the idea that some people should be involved in full-scale evangelism, while others do discipling. I do not see the need for radically separating these ministries, as will be noted in my chapter on the mandate. Making disciples as a lifestyle, in my view, should characterize every believer, including those specially engaged in evangelizing the unreached masses.

recurring themes of our Lord's resurrection message to the church: His affirmation (Matt. 28:18); His mandate (Matt. 28:19, 20); and His promise (Matt. 28:20). As an epilogue, the ultimate question of Jesus is posed: " 'Do you love me?' " (John 21:15–19).

A work of this brevity, of course, cannot cover every aspect of the subject. Many areas of interest to missiologists are only touched on or passed over altogether. My concern has not been to present an exhaustive treatise on missions, but simply to lift up the basic thrust of the Great Commission as it relates to our lives today.

I have sought to let the inerrant Scripture speak for itself, without undue recourse to secondary authorities. However, in the study, I have not hesitated to consult the work of scholars who have written in the field. For those who would like to pursue the subject further, the bibliographic references that appear in footnotes may prove helpful.

What is set forth in these pages was originally prepared for oral presentation at college and seminary assemblies.[13] Since I was working within rather limited perimeters of time in these settings, I have tried to reduce the message to basic issues, while keeping the thought moving, aware that students' attention level can be easily overestimated.

Much of the content will be found in other of my writings, though doubtless it is more concentrated in this format.[14] In

---

13. These presentations include the George Peter's Lectures at Dallas Theological Seminary and the Chandler Lectures at the Officers Training College of the Salvation Army in New York. In an earlier form, they were given in the Stanley Distinguished Speakers Lectures at Wheaton College.

14. Of particular relevance are my studies on the life of Christ, *The Master Plan of Evangelism* and *The Mind of the Master*, as well as the sequel in the Acts of the Apostles, *The Master Plan of Discipleship*, all published by Fleming H. Revell Co. Some of the theological issues are addressed in *The Heartbeat of Evangelism* and *The New Covenant*, published by NavPress. Mention might be made, too, of *Songs of Heaven*, also published by Revell.

a sense, these reflections encapsulate my philosophy of ministry—convictions that have grown through the years as I have
tried, however falteringly, to conform my life to the priorities
of the Kingdom and the guidelines of the Great Commission.

After you have read each part, you may want to turn over
some of the ideas in your mind. Even better, a few others
might get together with you to interact with the text. To
encourage such reflection a study guide is provided at the end
of the text.

Going Out With God

I will never forget one day before my dad died, he turned to
me and asked, "Son, where does a man go when he goes out
with God?"

The question came as a surprise, and I was at a loss for an
answer. Seeing my perplexity, Dad smiled, and then in a
quiet voice said, "Well, does it matter? You just go wherever
He wants to go. There is nothing to worry about, for He
knows the way."

Dad was thinking of that passage in Scripture that says of
Abraham: ". . . when he was called to *go out* into a place
which he should after receive for an inheritance, obeyed; and
he went out, not knowing whither he went. By faith he so-
journed in the land of promise, as in a strange country, dwell-
ing in tabernacles with Isaac and Jacob, the heirs with him of
the same promise. For he looked for a city which hath foundations, whose builder and maker is God" (Heb. 11:8–10 KJV,
italics mine).

That is how it is when we "go out" with Jesus. It is not our
place to tell Him where to take us or to suit His summons to
our convenience; our part is to obey—to stake everything we
are and everything that we have upon His honor and faithfulness. Yes, the journey will be tedious, attended with many

trials and dangers, but we need not fear what our future holds. He knows the way, and in His own time He will bring us into "the city which has foundations"—that destiny of the redeemed where the heirs of Abraham, numerous as the stars in heaven, serve the King in perfect love and eternal praise (Gal. 3:29).

The Great Commission calls us to measure our lives now by this heavenly vision. *Whatever does not contribute to its fulfillment is an exercise in futility.* So looking to Jesus, let us "go out" to claim our inheritance. The best is yet to be! We are on our way to a great reunion with all the saints of light, when we shall behold our Lord in the glory of His Kingdom.

The Great Commission Lifestyle

Part One
The Affirmation

"All authority in heaven and on earth has been given to me."

Matt. 28:18

For there is one God and one mediator between God and men, the man Christ Jesus, who gave himself as a ransom for all men. . . .

1 Tim. 2:5, 6

Assurance of Authority

Where we begin in world evangelism largely determines where we will end.[1] If we begin with the human predicament, there is little to keep us from ending in frustration, if not despair. But if we start with God, with our attention fixed on things above, where Christ reigns in eternal triumph, the vision of His glory inspires us to greater resolve and confidence.

The people about to receive the command to disciple all nations needed this higher perspective. They had come through the shattering experience of their Lord's betrayal and crucifixion. In the trauma of those events, at one point the disciples all left Him and fled into the night (Mark 14:50, 52; Matt. 26:56).

Then they confronted the astounding news that Jesus had risen from the dead. The transcendence of the resurrection over everything in the natural realm of law and forces staggered their faith. Indeed, when first told by Mary that Jesus was alive, the disciples "did not believe it" (Mark 16:11); nor could they believe the testimony of the two men who had walked with Jesus on the Emmaus Road and broken bread with Him in their home (Luke 24:13–35; Mark 16:12, 13). That evening when He appeared to the apostolic company, except Thomas, the disciples were "startled and frightened, thinking they saw a ghost" (Luke 24:37). Rebuking their "lack of faith," Jesus showed them His nail-pierced hands and feet and invited an inspection of His wounds (Mark 16:14;

---

1. Grateful acknowledgment is made to the *Journal of the Academy for Evangelism in Theological Education*, where this chapter is included in vol. 6, 1991. A condensed version also appeared in the *Trinity World Forum* 16, no. 2 (Winter 1991).

Luke 24:36–43; John 20:19–25). The next Sunday He gave Thomas the same opportunity, telling him to " 'stop doubting and believe' " (John 20:27; cf. 20:26–31).[2]

Jesus understands the human desire for scientific evidence and, with intuitive sympathy yet firmness, ministers to those struggling with honest doubt. This may explain why, over a period of forty days, in various places and at different times, He showed Himself to the disciples and "gave many convincing proofs that he was alive" (Acts 1:3).[3]

As the time approaches for Jesus to return to heaven, the disciples gather on the mountain "where Jesus had told them to go" (Matt. 28:16).[4] Indicative of their deep affection, "when they saw him, they worshipped him"; yet in this display of their adoration, we are told that "some doubted" (Matt. 28:17).[5]

Why there would be doubt now in the minds of "some"

---

2. The Gospel writers make no attempt to hide the disciples' incredulous tendency, particularly regarding the resurrection. This only adds authenticity to the account and actually makes it easier to identify with them, for the disciples are seen to be persons with the same human foibles as ourselves.

3. There are ten recorded instances of Jesus appearing to His disciples in His resurrection body, prior to His ascension. Altogether more than five hundred people saw Him, most of whom were still alive at the time Paul wrote the Corinthian letter (1 Cor. 15:6). Significantly, though, there is no reference to Jesus ever appearing to confirmed unbelievers, which underscores the principle of His concentration upon persons who wanted to follow Him. For a good discussion of the evidences of the resurrection, *see* Frank Morison, *Who Moved the Stone?* (Grand Rapids, Mich.: Zondervan, 1958) and R. T. France, *The Evidence for Jesus* (Downers Grove, Ill.: InterVarsity Press, 1986).

4. The site of this mountain is not indicated, leading to various conjectures as to its location. My own feeling is that it probably was the same place in Galilee where earlier He had been transfigured (Matt. 17:1–13; Mark 9:2; Luke 9:28). Notwithstanding its location, that it was a mountain would have awakened memories of other occasions when Jesus manifested His divine authority (e.g., Matt. 4:8–10; 5:1, 2; 15:29–31; 24:3).

5. The word *doubt* here does not imply unbelief but confusion or perplexity. Only in Matt.14:31 is the word used elsewhere in the New Testament, there in connection with Jesus walking on the water, when Peter became afraid and doubted. A beautiful treatment of this text is by G. Campbell Morgan, *The Missionary Manifest* (Grand Rapids, Mich.: Baker Book House, 1970, first published 1909), 41–43.

disciples is not explained. Perhaps they were overwhelmed by the wonder of it all. Their faith, though sincere, may still have been weak and halting. More likely, however, I suspect their qualms concerned their own ability to live up to the expectations of their Lord, an anxiety intensified by the awareness that He was soon to leave them.

For whatever reason there was doubt, "Jesus came to them . . ." (Matt. 28:18). Isn't that just like Him? He sees our need for reassurance; He knows how we wrestle with inferiority and fear. So, as in the other accounts of the Great Commission,[6] He assures them of His power before telling the disciples what to do.

His statement on this occasion covers everything. " 'All authority in heaven and on earth has been given to me' " (Matt. 28:18). In one sweeping declaration, He dispels any uncertainty in their minds about His ability to handle any situation. He has absolute sovereignty; His authority reaches across the vast expanse of the planet and unto the farthest star.[7]

Further confirming to His disciples the reality of His power, soon after giving the Great Commission (Matt. 28:19, 20), "he was taken up before their very eyes, and a cloud hid him from their sight" (Acts 1:9; cf. Mark 16:19; Luke 24:51).[8] His sacrificial ministry thus finished on earth,

---

6. Both John and Luke record Jesus speaking "peace" to His disciples before giving His commission (John 20:21; Luke 24:36), whereas Mark's version of Jesus' promise of powerful signs accompanying believers serves much the same purpose (Mark 16:17, 18).

7. All too easily we rush into the action mandate of the commission without pausing to consider what Jesus says first. I agree with Dr. Donald McGavran that the part of the Great Commission we are most prone to forget is Christ's declaration of authority. Arthur F. Glasser, "My Last Conversation With Donald McGavran," *Evangelical Missions Quarterly* 27, no. 1 (January 1991), 59.

8. The time interval between the commission in Matthew and Christ's ascension is not specified, but probably a period of a few days elapsed. When it happened makes no difference to the principle noted here.

and henceforth no longer confined by the limitations of space and time, He went back to take His place of authority at the right hand of God. There He reigns in unapproachable majesty, awaiting the day when He shall return to judge the living and the dead and to reign over His Kingdom forever.

Confronting the Gospel

With penetrating force, Christ's invincible authority, manifest in His resurrection and ascension, now makes the world answer for what happened at Calvary. *There must be some explanation for the cross.* For when a man dies who has power over death, then in all honesty one must ask: Why did He die in the first place?

To this unavoidable question, the Bible offers only one answer: "He was delivered over to death for our sins and was raised to life for our justification" (Rom. 4:25). Christ "bore our sins in his body on the tree, so that we might die to sins and live for righteousness . . ." (1 Pet. 2:24).

The late Robert G. Lee liked to tell about his visit to the Holy Land, when the guide of the touring party pointed in the distance to the place called Calvary. Seeing it for the first time, Dr. Lee's excitement was so great that he started to run up the hill. The guide was the first to catch up with him, finding him on the summit, his head bowed, still panting for breath. "Sir, have you been here before?" he asked.

For a moment there was a throbbing silence. Then in whispered awe, Dr. Lee replied, "Yes. I was here nearly two thousand years ago."

Indeed, we were all there nearly two thousand years ago. When Jesus died on that cross, He took our place. We had all turned to our own way, and the penalty of sin is death (Rom. 3:23; 6:23). Yet " 'God so loved the world' " that He gave His Son to die for us, even "while we were still sinners" (John 3:16; Rom. 5:8). As our representative, He suffered for us. ". . . the just for the unjust, in order that He might bring us to God, having been put to death in the flesh, but made alive in the spirit" (1 Pet. 3:18 NAS).

This is the gospel of salvation—the amazing news that the Creator and Lord of the universe has intervened in human history and, through the mighty conquest of Jesus Christ, made a way whereby ". . . whoever believes in him shall not perish but have eternal life" (John 3:16).

Centrality of Christ

The redemption of mankind clearly centers in the person and work of God's incarnate Word. "For just as through the disobedience of the one man [Adam] the many were made sinners, so also through the obedience of the one man [Jesus] the many will be made righteous" (Rom. 5:19; cf. 5:12–21). Though God's love extends to all nations, it ultimately focuses in His only begotten Son. "For there is one God and one mediator between God and men, the man Christ Jesus, who gave himself as a ransom for all men" (1 Tim. 2:5).

Think of what this means! To realize, as Paul said to the Colossians:

> He is the image of the invisible God, the firstborn over all creation. For by him all things were created: things in heaven and on earth, visible and invisible, whether thrones or powers or rulers or authorities; all things were created by him and for him. He is before all things, and in him all things hold together. . . . He is the beginning

and the firstborn from among the dead, so that in everything he might have the supremacy. For God was pleased
to have all his fullness dwell in him, and through him to
reconcile to himself all things, whether things on earth or
things in heaven, by making peace through his blood,
shed on the cross.

Col. 1:15–20; cf. 2:9–15

Having, therefore, completed once and for all His redemptive mission, "God exalted him to the highest place and gave
him the name that is above every name, that at the name of
Jesus every knee should bow, in heaven and on earth and
under the earth, and every tongue confess that Jesus Christ is
Lord, to the glory of God the Father" (Phil. 2:9–11; cf. Eph.
1:20–23).

This affirmation of His exalted position of authority re-
sounds through the witness of the apostolic church. "Jesus is
Lord!"[9] More than one hundred times He is identified by this
term in the Book of Acts alone.[10]

Peter's sermon on the day of Pentecost is a good example
(Acts 2:16–39). Having spoken of Christ's death, resurrec-
tion, and exaltation at the right hand of God, he concludes:
" 'Therefore let all Israel be assured of this: God has made

---

9. Probably this simple statement constituted the first creed of the Christian church,
as might be inferred from Rom. 10:9. Other confessions of faith may be reflected in
Matt. 16:16; 20:31; and 1 Cor. 15:3, 4. We should keep in mind, of course, that the
writings of the New Testament, which were being circulated from this time onward,
constituted a full composition of doctrine. For more information, see Oscar Cullman,
The Earliest Christian Confessions (London: Lutterworth Press, 1949).

10. If other terms were counted that imply lordship, like prince or judge, the number
of references to this position would be considerably greater. The title Lord, as
C. F. D. Moule points out, takes on more of a transcendental meaning in Acts,
gaining its significance in a demonstrated way through the resurrection. "The Chris-
tology of Acts," Studies in Luke-Acts, ed. Leander E. Keck and J. Louis Martyn
(Nashville, Tenn.: Abingdon Press, 1966), 161.

this Jesus, whom you crucified, both Lord and Christ' " (Acts 2:36; cf. 5:31; 10:36; Rom. 14:9).[11]

To the question "What must I do to be saved?" the answer was unequivocal: "Believe in the Lord Jesus" (Acts 16:30, 31). It was expected, too, that this faith in the lordship of Jesus be confessed with the mouth (Rom. 10:9, 10). The invitation to receive Christ was to all, but whoever responded called on "the name of the Lord" (Acts 2:21; Rom. 10:13).

Lord God Almighty

To identify Jesus by the title *Lord* is to declare that He is "God, the blessed and only Ruler," the King of glory (1 Tim. 6:15; John 20:28; Rev. 17:14). It is to affirm with Jesus that He " 'has all authority in heaven and on earth' " (Matt. 28:18).

In this sovereign power, while He was among us in the flesh He taught the Word of God (Matt. 7:24–29; John 12:49, 50; 14:24); He forgave sins (Matt. 9:2, 3; Mark 2:5–7; Luke 5:20, 21); He commanded devils to flee (Mark 1:27, 28; Luke 4:35–37); He wrought miracles (e.g., Matt. 9:25; Luke 7:15; John 11:44); and He promised to send the Holy Spirit (John 14:26; Luke 24:49; Acts 1:4, 5). Jesus lived in the consciousness of deity. He spoke of His heavenly origin (John 8:23) and the glory enjoyed with the Father before the world was made (John 17:5). Asserting His perfection, He pointed out that no one could accuse Him of sin (John 8:46). All His deeds were claimed to be the works

---

11. I have no inclination to enter into the debate surrounding lordship salvation. However, obviously, I stand with those who believe that in receiving Christ as Savior we also submit to Him as Lord. A competent treatment of this issue is by John F. MacArthur, Jr., *The Gospel According to Jesus* (Grand Rapids, Mich.: Zondervan, 1988).

of God (e.g., John 5:17; 10:14, 15; 14:11). With unassuming
frankness, He identified Himself as the Son of Man, who
commanded heavenly hosts (e.g., Matt. 13:41; 16:27). In
the same manner, He asked His followers to give Him the
devotion they would give to God (e.g., Matt. 10:37, 39),
and He accepted their worship.[12]

Not surprisingly, then, salvation is equated with knowing
the Son of God, whom to know aright is life everlasting. " 'I
am the way and the truth and the life,' " Jesus said. " 'No one
comes to the Father except through me' " (John 14:6). Not
only does He exclude other options, but He affirms that God
has " 'granted him authority over all people that he might
give eternal life to all those' " given Him (John 17:2). Defin-
ing what this means, Jesus prays: " 'This is eternal life: that
they may know you, the only true God, and Jesus Christ,
whom you have sent' " (John 17:3).

The destiny of mankind turns on the way men and
women believe these claims. Christ sets Himself before us,
not only as the object of our faith, but as the sole means of
salvation. Moreover, Jesus said that God "has entrusted all
judgment to the Son, that all may honor the Son just as they
honor the Father. He who does not honor the Son does not
honor the Father, who sent him" (John 5:22, 23; cf. 3:18;
5:27).

To many persons this teaching of Christ seems arrogant.
"What right does He have to impose His way upon others?"
they ask.

---

12. It is not necessary here to discuss the mystery of the incarnation of God and man
in the Person of Christ. However, suffice to say, that Christ acquired His personality
by virtue of union with God through conception of the Holy Spirit. Within His own
unique selfhood, the divine and human natures of Christ each retain their respective
properties and functions, without either alteration of essence or interference with the
other. The important truth is to realize that Christ possessed two natures, but only
one personality. The varying modes of consciousness may pass quickly from the
divine to the human, but the person is always the same.

A man once said to Dr. R. A. Torrey, "I'm not a Christian, but I am moral and upright. I would like to know what you have against me."

Torrey looked the man in the eye and with compassion replied: "I charge you, sir, with treason against heaven's king."[13]

The evangelist's retort may sound harsh, but isn't that the issue that must be faced? If, indeed, Jesus is God incarnate, with all authority in heaven and earth, should not every creature acknowledge Him and every tongue declare His praise?

Judgment Upon Unbelief

Notwithstanding the unbelief of the world, ". . . there is no other name under heaven given to men by which we must be saved" (Acts 4:12). For as the church has affirmed from the beginning, "there is but one God, the Father, from whom all things came and for whom we live; and there is but one Lord, Jesus Christ, through . . . whom we live" (1 Cor. 8:6).

Many persons, of course, will honor Him as one of the great religious leaders of the world, like a prophet, even perhaps the most noble man who ever lived; but those who insist that He is Lord and that He alone has the key to eternal life may have their claim dismissed with a chuckle, if not disdain. Resentment rises even more to the surface when reference is made to the judgment of God upon unbelief.

The popular notion, encouraged by our pluralistic society, is that it does not matter what one believes about Christ, for all

13. R. A. Torrey, *Great Gospel Sermons* vol. 1 (New York: Fleming H. Revell Co., 1949), 138.

roads lead to God, and ultimately everyone will be saved.[14]
God is viewed as too kind to sentence anyone to hell, or con-
versely, people are too nice to be damned. In either case, the
teachings of Christ regarding retribution for sin are naively cir-
cumvented, while the atoning purpose of His death is effec-
tively denied.

The fact is that the preaching of the cross and all that it
entails in the finality of Christ's saving work runs counter to
the wisdom of prideful men and women. It cuts across the
grain of our self-righteousness; it lays bare the arrogance of
our pretended independence. Anyone renouncing his own
rights, who comes to Jesus in true repentance and faith, can
expect to be called a fool (1 Cor. 1:17—2:14; 3:18–23; 4:10).

One has to ask, however, if it makes no difference how we
accept the authority of Christ, why preach the gospel? Does
not evangelism become superfluous?

Whatever our opinion may be, Jesus taught, " 'When the
Son of Man comes in his glory' " all people will be gathered
before Him in judgment (Matt. 25:31; cf. 11:22; 12:36). In
that day the wicked will be severed from the just (Matt.
13:49; cf. 24:40; Luke 17:34) as a shepherd divides his
sheep from the goats (Matt. 25:32, 46) or as wheat is separated from the tares (Matt. 13:30). Those who follow the
course of this world will be "thrown" into darkness (Matt.
8:12; 22:13; 25:30; Luke 13:28); assigned to "eternal pun-
ishment" (Matt. 25:46); and "cursed" into the hell of fire
prepared for the devil and his angels (Matt. 25:41; cf.

---

14. Not all proponents of religion have this universalistic assumption, of course.
Some, like Muslims, are quite adamant in their own exclusivistic beliefs. What it
means to be saved also may be variously understood. Hindus and Buddhists, as well
as devotees of the new age movement, for example, look upon the ultimate blessing
as the loss of self-identity in some kind of absorption with a great cosmic nirvana. The
kind of popular universalism that I refer to here is not so much an espoused faith, but
more of a religious indifference to any absolutes—a humanistic philosophy that per-
vades our whole culture.

5:22, 29, 30; 10:28; 18:9; 23:15, 33; Mark 9:43, 45, 47; Luke 12:5).

The Unreached World

But what about those multitudes who have never had the opportunity to hear the gospel—more than half the world's population, living in the bondage of false religion or idolatrous materialism? Will they be judged by the sincerity of their own quest for salvation through general revelation?

The problem with this view is that sincerity does not change error. And who has ever perfectly responded to all the light he has, to know God through the natural world? That is why the Scriptures conclude that everyone is "without excuse" and given over "to a depraved mind"[15] (Rom. 1:20, 28; cf. 1:18–32; 2:14, 15).

Let it be understood, though, that God " 'accepts men from every nation who fear him and do what is right' " (Acts 10:34, 35). To those who truly seek Him and walk in the light they have, He is pleased to give more light (Matt. 7:7; 13:12; Mark 4:25; Luke 11:9; cf. Rev. 3:20; Jer. 29:13). So responsibility for salvation rests with each individual.

Does this mean that one can be saved without a knowledge of Christ? To this, I can only answer that if such an alternative exists, it has not been disclosed to us. God, within His own

---

15. The limits of this presentation do not permit a full discussion of all the issues. For a summary of the problem, with a brief overview of its recent development in the church, *see* Kenneth S. Kantzer, "The Claims of Christ and Religious Pluralism," *Evangelism on the Cutting Edge*, ed. Robert E. Coleman (Old Tappan, N. J.: Fleming H. Revell Co., 1986), 15–28. An excellent popular treatment of the subject from the standpoint of missions is by Robert McQuilkin, *The Great Omission* (Grand Rapids, Mich.: Baker, 1984). For a penetrating assessment of the whole question of judgment, including eternal separation of the lost in relation to God's desire for all people to be saved, there is no better treatment than Ajith Fernando's recent study *Crucial Questions About Hell* (Eastbourne, England: Kingsway Pubs., 1991).

nature, can do whatever He pleases, but I can act only on the basis of His revealed Word.

That is why we dare not hesitate or spare any cost to bring the gospel to the unreached peoples of the earth. Though not their judge, we do know that they are lost without hope and doomed to hell. To ignore their plight would bring into question how deeply we take to heart the message of Christ.

When Charles Peace, the infamous criminal, was offered by the prison chaplain "the consolations of religion" on his way to the scaffold, the wretched man turned upon him, and exclaimed: "Do you believe it? Do you believe it?" Then, with obvious bitterness, he cried: "If I believed that, I would crawl across England on broken glass on my hands and knees to tell men it was true."[16]

Indeed, if we believe that Jesus is Lord, and that He died to bring redemption to all people, then we cannot sit by idly while multitudes perish. Knowing what is at stake, we must do for them what we would want them to do for us, were we in their place.

Spiritual Warfare

We can expect opposition. The claims of Jesus always conflict with the aspirations of Satan. This pretender to the throne of Christ, having been cast from heaven, never rests in his effort to usurp the authority of Christ.[17] Challenging the rule of

---

16. Quoted by G. Ray Jorden, *The Supreme Possession* (New York: Abingdon-Cokesbury, 1945), 45.
17. Satan, once an exalted creature in heaven, appears to have tried to usurp a place of rule at the throne of God. A struggle ensued, and he and his cohorts were cast down to earth (Rev. 12:7–9; Luke 10:18). Though the power of the pretender has been broken, for a period he has been permitted by God to exercise influence in the kingdoms of this world (Luke 4:6; John 12:31; 16:11). One may wonder why God did not immediately cast Satan into hell, knowing that he would beguile men and women

Satan means warfare, not against flesh and blood, but against diabolical principalities of evil and spiritual wickedness that reach into high places (Eph. 6:12).

Nowhere will the satanic attack become more determined than in evangelism. That is where the issue of authority is decided. Knowing that his kingdom of darkness is threatened, the devil seeks to remove the good seed of the gospel (Matt. 13:19); he sows seeds of discord (Matt. 13:38, 39); he blinds the eyes of unbelievers (2 Cor. 4:4). Like a roaring lion, "the prince of this world" prowls about "looking for someone to devour" (John 14:30; 1 Pet. 5:8). Make no mistake about it. Turning people "from the power of Satan to God" involves mortal combat with the evil one (Acts 26:18). Every advance of the gospel will have to be won by conquest.

The contest becomes intense when we encounter other religions. Though these ideologies may provide some meaning to the lives of their adherents, insofar as they divert final authority from Christ, they reflect the deception of the evil one. There are areas where we have common ground with devotees of other faiths, of course, and we should seek in humility and compassion to build bridges of understanding; but let us be realistic about the demonic treachery that beguiles their souls.

The conspiracy of evil has infiltrated all the power structures of society, including governments, schools, business conglomerates, social agencies, even the organized church. No institution fallen creatures have developed escapes the enemy's cunning. Working through misguided subjects and

---

to sin. Though no answer can take away the mystery, still it can be observed that the demonic presence in this world now creates a situation whereby we—through anguish, especially in vicarious relationships—can learn even greater depths of holy love. As the ultimate cause of all sin, then, the devil actually fulfills a beneficial function in the divine economy. In the final triumph of judgment, of course, Satan will be removed to hell.

the systems of this world and using whatever devious means expedient—slander, intrigue, deceit, rebellion, betrayal, intimidation, and infliction of torture—the devil seeks to destroy the work of Christ. There are indications, too, that his attacks upon the servants of God will become more brazen and murderous as the end of the age approaches (Rev. 12:12).

Triumph of the Kingdom

But we need not fear the fury of the adversary. Greater is He who lives in the saints than the manipulator of the world (1 John 4:4). Jesus has all authority, not Satan. The time is hastening when all the powers of this age shall be put under His feet (Matt. 22:44; Acts 2:35; Heb. 1:13; 10:13). If, then, Christ is for us, who can be against us? In Him we are more than conquerors (Rom. 8:31, 37).

Disciples of the cross engage the enemy in this assurance of victory. The church of God, like an undefeatable army, will at last shatter the strongholds of Satan and storm the gates of hell. Whatever the struggles in this present age, we know that nothing can ultimately prevail against Zion's King. He already reigns in the hearts of those who worship Him, and the day is coming when He shall take dominion over His creation. The affirmation of the Great Commission points to this glorious consummation of history, to which all things are moving, when finally:

> Jesus shall reign where'er the sun
> Does his successive journeys run;
> His kingdom spread from shore to shore
> Till moons shall wax and wane no more.[18]

18. From the hymn by Isaac Watts, "Jesus Shall Reign Where'er the Sun."

Confident of their Lord's ascent to the throne of glory and empowered by His Spirit, the disciples went forth boldly to herald the gospel to the ends of the earth.[19] They were convinced that God's redeeming grace extended to " 'all people,' " even to peoples " 'who are far off' " (Acts 2:17, 39; cf. Joel 2:28–32; Eph. 2:13, 17). In Christ there was "neither Jew nor Greek, slave nor free, male nor female" (Gal. 3:28). All who come to Him "are Abraham's seed, and heirs according to the promise" (Gal. 3:29; cf. Acts 3:25; 26:6; 28:20). What the Creator planned in the beginning, when "from one man he made every nation of men . . ." (Acts 17:26), thus, finds realization in the coming Kingdom, a message resounding again and again through the preaching of Peter, Stephen, Philip, Paul, and all the other apostolic witnesses (Acts 2:30; 3:21; 7:55; 8:12; 14:22; 19:8; 20:25; 28:23). Through the transforming power of the Word and the Spirit, a day was envisioned when the completed church, the bride of Christ, would be presented faultless before the presence of His glory with exceeding joy (Jude 24).

Celebration in Heaven

This is what John saw when, caught up in the Spirit, he looked through the door of heaven and beheld that great worshiping host before the throne of God (Rev. 4:1, 2).[20] Joined

---

19. Prior to the Lord's ascension to heaven and the confirming witness of His Spirit at Pentecost (Acts 2:33), the comprehensive nature of the Kingdom seemed difficult for the disciples to grasp (e.g., Matt. 19:27, 28; 20:21; Luke 17:20, 21; 24:21; Acts 1:4, 5). Like their Jewish contemporaries, they tended to think of God's blessing only in terms of Israel. It would appear that embracing the full extent of Christ's authority is one result of being full of His Spirit.

20. The revelation John was given by God is intended to show His servants what will take place (Rev. 1:1). In unveiling the reigning Christ, the account depicts His conquest over every kind of opposition and the establishment of His eternal King-

with the seraphim and cherubim (Rev. 4:6–8; 5:8, 14; 7:11; 19:4), the elders (Rev. 4:4, 10; 5:8, 14; 7:11; 11:16; 19:4), and myriads of angels (Rev. 5:11, 12; 7:11), he sees the assembly of the saints, great and small, gathered from the foundation of the world. They are clothed in white robes and are holding palm branches in their hands.[21] Their number is so great that no one can count them. As far as the eye can see in every direction—from the east and the west, from the north and from the south—they are gathered. They come "from every nation, tribe, people and language" (Rev. 7:9; cf. 12:10; 15:2, 3).

The Great Commission is fulfilled! In the schedule of eternity, it is already accomplished; the celebration has begun. Hallelujahs of the victorious church are ringing through the courts of heaven. A mighty shout can be heard, saying: " 'Salvation belongs to our God, who sits on the throne, and to the Lamb' " (Rev. 7:10).

Do you hear them? With "loud voices," they cry: " 'The kingdom of the world has become the kingdom of our Lord and of his Christ, and he will reign for ever and ever' " (Rev. 11:15).

Listen! They are singing: " 'Now have come the salvation and the power and the kingdom of our God, and the authority of his Christ. For the accuser of our brothers . . . has been hurled down. They overcame him by the blood of the Lamb

dom. While much of the narrative concerns the destructive work of evil on the earth and the consequent judgments that fall upon the wicked, occasionally the scene shifts to heaven, and we get a glimpse of Him who sits on the throne and the celebration of His triumph by the worshiping hosts. These reoccurring visions of Christ's glory set the tone of the book and serve to remind the church that He who has all authority is directing the unfolding destiny of the nations.

21. The white robes worn by the saints not only depict their purity but also speak of victory, while the palm branches they hold indicate their triumphant joy. In this scene, they magnify their Lord, who has conquered, not through force of arms, as kings of the earth, but by giving Himself to die for the world.

and by the word of their testimony; they did not love their lives so much as to shrink from death' " (Rev. 12:10, 11).[22]

In the final acclamation of the saints at the marriage supper of the Lamb, they are shouting: " 'Hallelujah! Salvation and glory and power belong to our God, for true and just are his judgments' " (Rev. 19:1, 2). Again they shout, " 'Hallelujah' " (Rev. 19:3). The magnitude of their united voice is likened to "the roar of rushing waters," as though a hundred oceans were crashing the shore (Rev. 19:1, 6). Or to use another figure, the intensity of their victory shout is compared to "loud peals of thunder," splitting the heavens in rolling sonic booms, saying: " 'Hallelujah! For our Lord God Almighty reigns' " (Rev. 19:6).

Now the mission of the church on earth may seem slow and sometimes discouraging, but the ultimate triumph of evangelism is never in doubt. The King is coming! Someday the trumpet will sound, and the Son of Man, with His legions of angels, shall descend from heaven in trailing clouds of glory, and He shall reign over all, "Lord of lords and King of kings" (Rev. 17:14).

Living on Tiptoes

In an expedition to an unreached area the Reverend E. P. Scott, a pioneer missionary to India, once came upon a hostile band of warriors. They seized him and pointed their long spears at his heart. Feeling utterly helpless, but resting on the promises of God, the missionary drew out the violin that he

22. Perhaps I should note that for my purpose it is not necessary to determine the exact time this and other heavenly voices fit in the unfolding events of the last days. However one interprets the millennium and its related happenings, the voices about the throne are true. For a study of all these doxologies in the Book of Revelation, *see* my book *The Songs of Heaven* (Old Tappan: Fleming H. Revell Co., 1980).

carried with him and began to play and sing in the native language:

> All hail the power of Jesus' name!
> Let angels prostrate fall;
> Bring forth the royal diadem,
> And crown Him Lord of all.[23]

As the words rang out, Reverend Scott closed his eyes, momentarily expecting death. But when nothing happened, even after the third stanza, he opened his eyes and saw that the spears had fallen from the hands of his captors. Tears filled their eyes. The warriors pled with him to tell them of that name—the name above every name. So he went home with them, and for several years worked in their midst, winning many to Christ.[24]

I see in this story a parable for us today. Not that we will be delivered from adversity, even death, for God may want to seal our witness with blood. But whatever may come to us in the course of making disciples, the name of Christ shall finally prevail. God is working through every circumstance to accomplish His program. We shall overcome! While it does not yet appear what we shall be, "we know that when he appears, we shall be like him, for we shall see him as he is" (1 John 3:2). And every knee shall bow before Him and every tongue declare that Jesus Christ is Lord (Phil. 2:10, 11).

This is more than a creed; it is the glorious affirmation of our Lord Himself: " 'All authority in heaven and on earth has been given to me' " (Matt. 28:18). So let us pick up His

---

23. From the hymn by Edward Perronet, "All Hail the Power of Jesus' Name."
24. Recounted by Louis Albert Banks, *Immortal Hymns and Their Stories* (Cleveland: Burrows Brothers, 1898), 312, 313; also reprinted by Amos R. Wells, "All Hail the Power of Jesus' Name," *The Christian Endeavor World* (May 26, 1904).

shout, and in full assurance of faith, go forth to proclaim His glory to every creature, until,

> . . . With yonder sacred throng
>   We at His feet may fall!
> We'll join the everlasting song,
> And crown Him Lord of all.[25]

---

25. Perronet, "All Hail the Power."

Part Two
The Mandate

"Therefore go and make disciples of all nations, baptizing them in the name of the Father and of the Son and of the Holy Spirit, and teaching them to obey everything I have commanded you. . . ."

Matt. 28:19, 20

"This is to my Father's glory . . . showing yourselves to be my disciples."

John 15:8

A Required Course

The comic actor W. C. Fields was once found by a friend reading the Bible. Asked what he was doing, Fields replied, "Looking for loopholes."[1]

I suspect that is the way many of us have approached the last command of Christ to His disciples, particularly as it relates to the obligation of every believer to join Him in making disciples.

But try as we may, there are no loopholes. The mandate simply underscores a life-style incumbent upon the whole church.[2] There are no escape clauses, no substitute options. As we might say in the academic world, the Great Commission is not an elective course; it is part of the required curriculum.

---

1. Quoted by Robert M. Holmes, *Why Jesus Never Had Ulcers* (Nashville, Tenn.: Abingdon, 1986).
2. Though the Matthew text only mentions "the eleven disciples" (Matt. 28:16), the "some who doubted" may allude to others present (*see* Matt. 28:17). Probably, too, the "more than five hundred" brothers who saw Christ after His resurrection, noted by Paul, were present at this time (1 Cor. 15:6). *See* Samuel Zwemer, *Into All the World: The Great Commission—A Vindication and Interpretation* (Grand Rapids, Mich.: Zondervan, 1943), 93; David M. Howard, *The Great Commission for Today* (Downers Grove, Ill.: InterVarsity Press, 1976), 55; Robert D. Culver, "What Is the Church's Commission?" *Bibliotheca Sacra*, 125:499 (July-September, 1968), 240; and A. T. Robertson, who in addition to the Corinthian record, parallels Mark's account with that of Matthew, *A Harmony of the Gospels for Students of the Life of Christ* (New York: Harper & Brothers, 1922), 249. For the more limited view of the disciples present, *see* Karl Barth, "An Exegetical Study of Matthew 28:16–20," *The Theology of Christian Mission*, ed., G. H. Anderson (New York: McGraw Hill, 1961), 59. Regardless of who was present when the command was given, however, the case for believing every Christian must make disciples does not rest finally upon the number of persons who heard Jesus speak, but upon the nature of a disciple as a follower of the Lord.

His Command

The directive, issuing from Christ's authority, comes out in the action portion of the Commission: " 'Therefore go and make disciples of all nations, baptizing them in the name of the Father, and of the Son and of the Holy Spirit, and teaching them to obey everything I have commanded you . . .' " (Matt. 28:19, 20).

In the original text, there is but one verb, "make disciples." "Go," "baptizing," and "teaching" are participles, which means that these activities do not stand alone. As in English, so in Greek: Participles derive their force from the leading verb. The implications of this are quite significant for ministry, for it means that the reason for going anywhere, whether next door or across the ocean, is to make disciples.[3] Similarly, the evangelistic imperative to preach the gospel and to bring persons into baptism, aims to make followers of Christ, just as teaching has its objective in the building up of these disciples. *The whole thrust of the Great Commission—giving direction and validity to every effort—is the discipling of all nations.*

Notice that the command is not to make converts. In other contexts, of course, Jesus emphasizes the necessity of conversion (e.g., Matt. 18:3; John 3:1–36). Tragically, however, too many converts, if indeed they are born again, fail to go on with Jesus, and His plan for reaching the world through their witness is never realized. The irresponsible way that the church has accommodated this situation, I believe, explains why so much of the world's population still languishes in darkness.

---

3. As this sentence is constructed, the participle "go," however, does stand in a coordinate relationship with the verb, which gives it the force of an imperative. The rule also pertains to the mandate in Mark 16:15, where "go" is related to the imperative "preach the good news."

A *Disciple* means "learner or pupil," as in the sense of an apprentice.[4] Such a person is more than a convert, though turning to the Savior in repentance and faith certainly must take place. But disciples do not stop with conversion; they keep moving on with Christ, ever learning more of His grace and glory.

Here is the genius of His plan to win "all nations," raising up a people in His likeness. For disciples of Christ grow in His character, and by the same virtue, they develop in His life-style and ministry to the world. By making this the focal concern, Jesus assures an ever-enlarging labor force, and in time, through multiplication, workers will bring the good news to the ends of the earth.

Christ's disciples are only asked to live by the same rule that governed His time among us. That is what the commission is all about. It simply enunciates the strategy implicit in His own ministry while He was with us in the flesh. Just as the Lord ordered His life on earth, now His disciples are expected to follow in His steps.

His Visible Pattern

To understand what this means, we must look closely at the way Jesus made disciples. His pattern of doing it becomes the interpretation of the command. Though our understanding is encumbered with all the limitations of fallen intelligence, it is

---

4. The term *disciple* can be applied to any master-pupil relationship, and sometimes is so used in Scripture (e.g., Matt. 8:21, 22; John 6:66), but normally in the Gospels and in Acts it denotes persons who follow Christ. Implied in the word is "the criteria of a personal attachment which shapes the whole life of the one described." *Theological Dictionary of the New Testament*, ed. Gerhard Kittel, trans. and ed. Geoffrey W. Bromley, vol. 4 (Grand Rapids, Mich.: Wm. B. Eerdmans, 1967), 441; cf. Paul Sevier Minear, *The Images of the Church in the New Testament* (London: Littenworth, 1960), 145–48; and John F. MacArthur, Jr., *The Gospel According to Jesus* (Grand Rapids, Mich.: Zondervan, 1988), 196–202.

reassuring to know that in the Son of God we have a perfect teacher. He never made a mistake.

Adaptations of His approach to ministry, of course, must be made to our situation. The techniques Christ used in His culture, nearly twenty centuries ago, are not necessarily the same techniques He would use in our situation today. Methods are variable, conditioned by the time and circumstances, which are constantly changing. But principles, inherent in His way of life, never change. They provide guidelines for making disciples in every society and every age.

Becoming a Servant

One does not have to observe Jesus very long without being made aware that He lived by a different value system from that of the world. Renouncing His own rights, He "made himself nothing, taking the very nature of a servant, being made in human likeness" (Phil. 2:7). Though He possessed all the glory of God, ". . . he became poor, so that you through his poverty might become rich" (2 Cor. 8:9).

His lowly birth in a manger accented His chosen way of life (Luke 2:7). When it is considered that He is the only person ever born into this world who controlled the circumstances surrounding His life, it makes His decision the more startling.[5]

Most of His incarnate life was lived in obscurity in an unbecoming city, where He learned a carpenter's trade. The

---

5. Christ's coming into the world and the events of His life culminating at Calvary were decided in the council of the Godhead before the beginning of time (Rev. 13:8; cf. Acts 2:23). When He took the form of a servant in the incarnation, Jesus still retained His divinity, and in this nature He remained obedient to the ordained will of the Father (John 10:17, 18; 14:31; 15:10; Heb. 10:9). There were no accidents in His life; everything Christ said and did was in the plan of God before the stars were fixed in place.

earthly father of Jesus is not mentioned in the later portions of the Gospels, so it is generally assumed that Joseph must have died while Jesus was still a young man, probably in His teens. He was left with the responsibility for taking care of not only His mother, but also His younger brothers and sisters.[6] One may be sure that He experienced the struggle of raising a family.

At about the age of thirty, having fulfilled the obligations of the eldest son, Jesus left home to pursue His public career. He was then accosted by Satan and tempted with the allurements of the world. "Get what you deserve—turn stones into bread to satisfy your appetite, then jump off the pinnacle of the temple that the angels of God might lift you up," the archdeceiver taunted (*see* Matt. 4:1–7; Luke 4:1–4; 9–13). How these feats of power would have invoked the crowd's applause! In fact, Jesus was promised all the kingdoms of the earth, if He would only accommodate "the god of this age" (Matt. 4:8–10; 2 Cor. 4:4). But our Lord would not be diverted from His mission; His work cannot be accomplished by indulgence of the flesh, however legitimate the appeal.[7]

Jesus came to serve, and in that role He went about doing good. Whenever He saw need, "moved with compassion," He reached out to help (Matt. 9:36 KJV). He fed the hungry; He healed the sick; He opened the eyes of the blind; He cleansed the lepers; He bound up the brokenhearted; He delivered the demon possessed; He raised the dead. And through it all, He held forth the Word of Life, proclaiming the good news of the Kingdom.

Little wonder that multitudes were drawn to Him. People

---

6. Four brothers of Jesus are mentioned in Scripture, along with "his sisters" (Matt. 13:55, 56; cf. 12:46; Mark 3:31; John 2:12; 7:3, 5; 1 Cor. 9:5; Gal. 1:19).

7. In the case of Christ, His temptations all appealed to a legitimate desire. That is what makes them so beguiling. Probably no compromise of values is more difficult to resist than the idea that spiritual goals can be fulfilled in self-serving ways.

always respond to love, when it finds practical expression in ministry, the more so when it is empowered by the Spirit of God. Though His fearless preaching often invoked the disdain of the religious gentry, it generally was received with appreciation by the masses (Mark 12:12; Matt. 21:26; Luke 20:19). In fact, so great was veneration for Him among the common people that they once intended to "make him king by force" (John 6:15; cf. 3:26; 11:47, 48). Indicative of His popular following, the last time He entered Jerusalem, crowds turned out to welcome Him, shouting, " 'Hosanna! Blessed is he who comes in the name of the Lord' " (John 12:13).

Problem of the Multitudes

But as Jesus looked upon the city, tears filled His eyes, for He knew that the people did not really understand who He was, nor did they comprehend the Kingdom that He had come to establish (Luke 19:41–44).[8] They wanted a Messiah who would use His mighty power to overthrow their enemies and satisfy their temporal desires. Good people, generally respectful, they nevertheless were utterly self-serving in their interests. Neither the love of God nor the love of neighbor motivated their actions.

Making the situation worse, the masses had no one to show them the way. They were like aimless sheep without a shepherd (Matt. 9:36). Oh, yes, there were many leaders who were supposed to give direction, like the scribes and priests. The problem was that these persons were themselves blind to the truth (Matt. 15:14; Luke 6:39), nor did they truly love the

---

8. The consequences of their spiritual blindness made His anguish more unbearable, for Jesus could see the judgment coming upon the people because they " 'did not recognize the time of God's coming' " to them (Luke 19:44; cf. 19:29–44; Mark 11:1–11; Matt. 21:1–11, 14–17; John 12:12–19).

people. Jesus called them "hirelings"—persons who are only in it for what they get out of it. In the time of crisis, when the sheep were under attack, they would run away and leave the sheep prey to wolves (John 10:12, 13).

You can see why Jesus wept over Jerusalem. The multitudes were lost. Confused by their own waywardness and the victimization of self-serving religious professionals, they were an easy prey to the beguilements of Satan. When it appeared to them that Jesus would bring in a new era of freedom and prosperity, they were eager to declare His praise; but a few days later, when it was obvious that His Kingdom was not of this world, they cried, " 'Crucify him! Crucify him! We have no king but Caesar' " (Mark 15:11–15; Matt. 27:22–26; Luke 23:20, 21; John 19:15).

We blink our eyes in dismay, wondering how people can be so callous, so fickle in their allegiance. Of course, to openly take the side of Jesus in the judgment hall of Pilate would have meant retaliation from the chief priests and officers. It might have brought ostracism from the temple, perhaps even the loss of employment, if not arrest as a troublemaker. Under these conditions, it seemed expedient to play it safe and follow the crowd. What a commentary on human nature!

Understand it, for unless you come to grips with this condition, you will never be relevant to the Great Commission. A fundamental transformation must take place in the human heart, a change so radical that self-indulgent sheep become self-giving shepherds, willing, if necessary, to lay down their lives for the sake of others.

Concentrate on the Answer

For this to happen, the sheep must have shepherds to lead them. Jesus was doing all He could to help, but in the incarnation He assumed the limitation of His body. He could not give attention to all of the people. It was obvious that unless spiritual leaders could be raised up who could multiply His ministry—redeemed men and women with the heart of Christ—there was no way the waiting harvest could be gathered (Matt. 9:37, 38).

So while ministering to the multitudes, Jesus concentrated upon making some disciples who would learn to reproduce His life and mission. In doing so He loved the multitudes no less. Indeed, it was for the sake of the masses that He had to devote Himself to a few willing learners in order for the world ultimately to be reached.

His first disciples were found largely within His home environment in Galilee.[9] In culture, training, and religious orientation they had much in common.[10] To be sure, they were not generally the most socially astute people, perhaps not even the most religious. None of them, for example, appear to be members of the Levitical priesthood.[11] By any standard of sophisticated culture, they would be viewed as a rather unpromising aggregation of souls.

Yet Jesus saw in these untrained laymen the potential for turning the world upside down. In spite of their limitations,

9. Galilee was commonly looked upon as the backwoods part of the country. Interestingly, the only one of the twelve known to have come from the more cultured area of Jerusalem is Judas Iscariot.

10. As with Jesus, there is no indication that any of the twelve were "college graduates." Certainly our Lord does not depreciate scholarship. Later, some of the best-educated members of society followed Him, including Saul of Tarsus and Luke the physician. But in the beginning He took a course that made clear formal higher education is not essential to His mission.

11. This is quite surprising in view of the large number of priests in Israel. Josephus, a historian of that era, claims there were twenty thousand priests working at the temple (*The Life Against Apion*, vol. 1 [Cambridge, Mass.: Harvard University Press, 1926], 335). There were members of this order interested in Christ, as can be observed by their presence in the crowds, but not until after Pentecost do we see any of them publicly identifying with Him (Acts 6:7).

they were willing to follow Jesus. That is all He asked (John 1:43, 46; Mark 2:14; Matt. 4:19, 20; 9:9; Luke 5:27). Though often superficial in their comprehension of spiritual reality, with the exception of the traitor, they were teachable. Such persons can be molded into a new image.

Staying Together

As their numbers grew, Jesus appointed twelve to be "with him" in a special apostleship (Mark 3:14).[12] He continued to relate to others as the fellowship of believers increased through His ministry, but it is apparent that He gave a diminishing priority of attention to those outside the apostolic circle. In this select group, Peter, James, and John seemed to enjoy an even closer relationship to the Master.

All this impresses me with the deliberate way that Jesus invested His life in persons in training. It also illustrates a basic principle of teaching: The more concentrated the size of the group being taught, the greater the opportunity for learning. In a profound sense, He is showing us how the Great Commission can become the controlling purpose of every family circle, every small group gathering, every close friendship in this life.

For the better part of three years, Jesus stayed with His pupils. Together they walked the highways and streets; together they sailed on the lake; together they visited friends; together they went to the synagogue and the temple; together they worked. Have you noticed that He seldom did anything alone? Imagine! He came to save the nations—and finally, He

---

12. Jesus went on to tell the disciples that He was sending them out "to preach and to have authority to drive out demons" (Mark 3:15). But we dare not forget that they were first ordained to be "with" Him. Their time together was the necessary preparation for the ministry to follow (cf. Mark 1:17; Matt. 4:19; Luke 5:10).

died on the cross for all mankind. Yet while here He spent
more time with a handful of disciples than with everybody
else in the world.

Giving an Example

In this close association, the disciples were given a demonstration of His mission. His life was the object lesson of His
doctrine. By practicing before them what He wanted them to
learn, they could see its relevance and application.

Take, for example, His habit of prayer. Surely it was no
accident that Jesus often let His disciples see Him conversing
with the Father. They could observe the priority of this spiritual discipline and the strength it gave to His life. Inevitably
the time came when they asked Him, " 'Lord, teach us to
pray . . .' " (Luke 11:1). They were ready to learn. Having
awakened their desire to pray, He could show them how.
Notice, though, in this beginning lesson, He did not preach
them a sermon or assign them a book to read; He gave them
an example (Luke 11:2–4; Matt. 6:9–13).

In the same way, He taught His disciples the importance
and use of Scripture, the meaning of worship, stewardship of
time and talents, social responsibility, and every other aspect
of His personal life. All the while, of course, He was showing
them how to care for the needs of people, bearing their sor-
rows, carrying their grief, ever seeking their ultimate welfare
in the gospel. In the process He was also demonstrating how
to make disciples, though it may not have dawned upon them
until they actually received the Great Commission.

Getting Them Involved

As they were able to assume responsibility, He got them involved in activities suited to their gifts. First duties were

small, unassuming tasks, like providing for the food and shelter of the group. Since Jesus was unmarried and had no house
of His own, it was natural for Him to accept graciously their
hospitality (Matt. 8:20; Mark 1:29; Luke 8:3). What a beautiful way to help some people get involved where they could
help! As far as I can find, our Lord never turned down an
invitation to dinner. I was glad when I discovered that!

After a while He began to have the disciples assist Him in
ministry. They were employed, for example, in baptizing persons who responded to His preaching (John 4:2).[13] In another
setting, He has them distributing food to hungry people who
came to hear Him (Mark 6:30–44; 18:1–9; Matt. 14:13–21;
15:29–38; Luke 9:10–17; John 6:1–13).

The work assignments increased with their developing self-
confidence and competence. Before long they were sent out
to do much the same kind of work that Jesus was doing with
them—healing, teaching, and preaching the gospel (Matt.
10:1–10; Mark 6:6–13; Luke 9:1–3; cf. 10:1–16). Lest they
forget the priority of training leadership, however, He stipu-
lated that above the public ministry they were to search out
"worthy" persons to spend time with, wherever they went
(Matt. 10:11–15; Mark 6:10, 11; Luke 9:4, 5).[14] In effect, the

---

13. It does not take a lot of theological training to know how to baptize somebody,
which may explain why the disciples were employed in this ritual, even before they
were officially ordained to preach. I must add, however, the particular way that Jesus
utilized disciples in His work need not be interpreted as a rule for all to follow today.
The principle of getting people involved is what matters, and the circumstances will
determine how it can be applied.

14. This "worthy" person was someone willing to receive the peace associated with
God's salvation. This person is not yet a disciple, but the Spirit of God has planted
in the heart a receptivity to the gospel, a desire to learn more of Christ. As the two
disciples stay in this house, mingling with those present, opportunity is given to win
other members of the household and so to form the nucleus for a new fellowship of
believers. So crucial was this plan to the disciples' ministry that if they could not find
a "worthy" house, they were to shake the dust off their feet and go to another village:
" 'It will be more bearable for Sodom and Gomorrah on the day of judgment than for
that town' " (Matt. 10:15). In retrospect, there is nothing new in this instruction.

disciples were told to concentrate upon the most promising
people, who would be able to follow up their ministry after
they were gone.

Continued Supervision

From time to time Jesus would get back with them and see
how things were coming along. Continually checking up on
their assignments, asking questions, responding to their que-
ries, He was building in them a sense of accountability. Experiences the disciples were having in ministry thus became
illustrations for Him to teach some new or deeper truth (e.g.,
Luke 9:37–43; 10:14–24; Matt. 15:37—16:12; 17:14–20;
Mark 8:10–21; 9:17–29. It was on-the-job training all the way.

Problems were dealt with as they came up, which was quite
often. Certainly the disciples were far from perfection, and
their spiritual immaturity was constantly coming out. To note
just one instance, recall the time James and John wanted to
call down fire on the heads of some disrespectful Samaritans
who refused them shelter (Luke 9:51–56). When Jesus saw
their impulsiveness, He rebuked them but also seized the
occasion to emphasize again the saving purpose of His mission. "You do not know what kind of spirit you are of, for the
Son of Man did not come to destroy men's lives, but to save
them" (Luke 9:55, 56).[15]

Here, as all the way through their training, the disciples
were pointed to the redemptive purpose of Christ's being in
the world and their function in continuing that mission.

Jesus is simply enunciating what He had already demonstrated in His own strategy of
concentrating upon persons who will someday become laborers in the harvest. For a
helpful discussion of this passage, *see* I. Howard Marshall, *Commentary on Luke* (Grand
Rapids, Mich.: W. B. Eerdmans, 1978), 419, 420.

15. This verse is not included in all the older manuscripts, so it may be relegated to
an alternate reading in our translations, as is the case with the NIV.

Though their progress was painfully slow, especially in comprehending the meaning of the cross, Jesus patiently kept them moving toward His goal. He did not ask more from them than they were capable of giving, but He did expect their best, and this He expected to improve as they continued to follow Him.

Reproduction of Life

Life inevitably reproduces its own kind. Careless persons who let the lusts of this world choke the Word of God will reap the folly of their ways. On the other hand, those living in conformity to Christ's Word develop the qualities of His life and ministry.

His parable of the vine and the branches is a beautiful illustration (John 15:1–17). Jesus likens Himself in this analogy to the vine and His disciples to the branches. The branches are conveyors of the life in the vine and, when properly functioning, produce a harvest. Any branch not fulfilling its purpose is cut off by the ever-watchful gardener. Even producing branches are pruned by the gardener in order that they will be more fruitful. " 'This is to my Father's glory,' " Jesus explained, " '. . . showing yourselves to be my disciples' " (John 15:8).

When fruit bearing is seen in this larger context of producing Christ-likeness, first in ourselves and then in others, practically everything Jesus did and said pointed to this truth. The Great Commission simply brings the principle into focus, phrasing it in terms of disciple making.

Jesus taught His followers to live with the harvest in view. " '. . . Open your eyes and look at the fields!' " He said, noticing the men coming to hear Him in Sychar. "They are ripe for harvest" (John 4:36).[16] The disciples could see what He meant and could also appreciate its spiritual application when He added, " 'Even now the reaper draws his wages, even now he harvests the crop for eternal life . . .' " (John 4:36). Whether they sowed or reaped, He wanted the disciples to realize that their work had impact upon eternity, ultimately culminating in the gathering of the nations at the throne of God.

The key to the final harvest is found in the quality and the supply of laborers obeying the mandate of Christ. It does not matter how few their numbers are in the beginning, provided that they reproduce and teach their disciples in turn to do the same. As simple as it may seem, this is the way His church will ultimately triumph. He has no other plan.

Our Lord did not come in His incarnate body to evangelize the world; He came to make it possible for the world to be saved through His atoning sacrifice. But on His way to Calvary, He made sure that His disciples were equipped by strategy and vision to gather the harvest.

A Pattern for His Church

He has given us a model that in principle every believer can follow. Too easily we have relegated His work to organized programs and special clerical vocations. Not that these ministries are unnecessary, for they are vital, and without them the church would not function as it does. But unless the Great Commission directs the daily life of the whole body, the church cannot function as it should.

---

16. Sometimes ripe grain is said to be "white . . . to harvest," as in the King James Version (John 4:35). Normally, ripe fields take on a golden hue. But if not gathered when ready, the grain will begin to turn white, which is an indication that the opportunity for harvesting is almost past. Unless reaped very soon, grain that has turned white will fall to the ground and will be lost.

Here the priesthood of all believers comes alive. Whatever our place of service, we live with a sense of destiny, knowing that each day moves us closer to consummation of the Kingdom. Making disciples is not a special calling or a gift of the Spirit; it is a life-style—the way that Jesus lived while He was among us and now the way He commands His people to follow.[17]

Begin Where You Are

Since this is best accomplished with a few people at any one time, at least in deep relationships, you will never lack an opportunity for ministry. You may be sure, too, that some of those who feel the warmth of your servant heart will also want to know more about your Lord.

Notice them. They are the answer to your prayers. Likely many of them will belong to your own peer group.

That reminds me of a man down in Texas who was arrested for horse stealing. The sheriff gave him the choice of being tried before the judge or a jury of his peers.

"Peers," he replied. "What's that?"

Whereupon the sheriff explained, "That means someone just like you."

"Well," said the man, "I'll take the judge. I don't want to be tried by a bunch of horse thieves."

---

17. In the last few years numerous authors have addressed the subject of discipleship. In addition to works already cited, including my own, consult Bill Hull, *Jesus Christ Disciple Maker* (Old Tappan, N. J.: Fleming H. Revell Co., 1984); Allen Coppedge, *The Biblical Principles of Discipleship* (Grand Rapids, Mich.: Zondervan, 1989); Matt Friedeman, *The Master Plan of Teaching* (Wheaton, Ill.: Victor Books, 1990); William A. Shell, *Come Follow Me* (Philadelphia: Great Commission Publications, 1988); and Keith Phillips, *The Making of a Disciple* (Old Tappan, N. J.: Fleming H. Revell Co., 1981). Add to this the writings of Leroy Eims, Carol Mayhall, Jack Mayhall, Roy Robertson, Dwight Pentecost, Carl Wilson, Beth Mainhood, Doug Hartman, Walter Henricksen, Christopher Adsit, Gary Kuhne, Myron Augsburger, David Dawson, Allen Hadidian, Juan Ortez, Ernest Best, Ajith Fernando, Ron Kincaid, Stanley Ott, Stuart Briscoe, and A. B. Bruce, among others.

If you look around, you will see persons with whom you already have much in common, beginning with your own family and reaching out from there to neighbors and friends. Within this natural sphere of influence, you will probably have the greatest potential for changing the world.[18]

With those persons who do not yet know the Savior, your relationship becomes a means of clarifying the gospel, bringing them to a place of decision.[19] The same servanthood pertains to believers needing encouragement and direction in their Christian life. Though you are not the only person responsible for their discipleship, for a period of time you may be one of the most significant influences in their Christian growth.

Learning Family Style

Like Jesus, you do it by being together. The more informal and unpretentious the association the better, like playing a round of golf. What a happy way to have some meaningful conversation! The exercise and recreation on the course is just a bonus. Who would ever want to play this game without the joy of fulfilling the Great Commission?

---

18. This principle is no less true when one is called to cross-cultural evangelism. In building bridges to gain a hearing for the gospel, a person drawn to you will more naturally come from those befriended through some relationship of concern. They in turn will be able to reach out to a larger group through their network of friends, and then the church will begin to multiply.

19. The way you led them to Christ likely will be the model they will try to emulate later. Remember that God works in different ways to draw people to Himself, and the approach that you use may not be the most effective method for another. Talk about it and help the disciple develop a personal method of evangelism with which he or she is comfortable. You can find guidance from many teachers such as: Paul Little, *How to Give Away Your Faith* (Chicago: InterVarsity Press, 1966); Bill Bright, *Witnessing Without Fear* (San Bernardino, Calif.: Here's Life Publishers, 1981); Howard Hendricks, *Say It With Love* (Ventura, Calif.: Gospel Light, 1972); Mark McCloskey, *Tell It Often—Tell It Well: Making the Most of Witnessing Opportunities* (San Bernardino, Calif.: Here's Life Publishers, 1986); and the compilation of twelve effective gospel communicators, Joel D. Heck, ed., *The Art of Sharing Your Faith* (Tarrytown, N. Y.: Fleming H. Revell Co., 1991), to mention only a few.

Such casual activities, of course, do not take the place of formal church services. Both are needed and serve the same purpose of making disciples. But learning comes more naturally in relaxed, familylike settings.

Some of this fellowship can be arranged in small-group meetings. These periods incorporate times of testimony, Bible study, prayer, or anything else deemed important to the participants.[20] In my own experience, for more than thirty years a meeting like this, every week, with a few students, at 6:30 A.M., has been one of the most rewarding disciplines of my life.

Such close association is especially crucial in preserving the fruit of evangelism. Like newborns in the physical world, beginning disciples must have spiritual guardians to help them in their Christian growth. Meet with them as often as possible, inquire about their needs, answer their questions, encourage their witness, and make them feel a part of the body of Christ.[21]

Give Disciples Something to Do

Maturing disciples with you might find in such follow-up a way to get involved in ministry. Many of the programs of the

20. Practical council on the formation and direction of small groups is readily available. If help is needed, the group programs prepared by Lyman Coleman are hard to beat for creative suggestions. Take a look at his *Encyclopedia of Serendipity* (Littleton, Colo.: Serendipity House, 1980), or from the same publisher, *The Serendipity Bible for Small Groups* (1990). For an introduction to the evangelistic possibilities of this approach, *see* Richard Peace, *Small Group Evangelism* (Nashville, Tenn.: Broadman Press, 1975); and Ralph Neighbor, *Where Do We Go From Here? A Guidebook for the Cell Group Church* (Houston, Tex.: Torch Publications, 1990).
21. Among the many introductions to follow-up, including guidelines of workable programs, are the books by Charlie Riggs, *Learning to Walk With God* (Minneapolis: World Wide Publications, 1986); Waylon B. Moore, *New Testament Follow-Up for Pastor and Laymen* (Grand Rapids, Mich.: Wm. B. Eerdmans, 1972); Gene Warr, *Making Disciples* (Fort Worth, Tex.: International Evangelism Assoc., 1986); and Gary Kuhne, *The Dynamics of Personal Follow-Up* (Grand Rapids, Mich.: Wm. B. Eerdmans, 1976). Above all, read Dawson Trotman's *Born to Reproduce* (Lincoln, Neb.: Back to the Bible, 1957).

church also afford opportunities for service. Early assignments can be in areas where they are already equipped, perhaps helping in the nursery or driving a bus. As they grow in grace and knowledge, disciples may assume leadership roles in the Sunday-school or youth activities, eventually becoming deacons and elders of the congregation.

According to their gifts and level of ability, all can do something. By the way, have you heard of that riding academy in West Texas that advertises that they have a horse to suit every taste? For fat people, they have fat horses; for skinny people they have skinny horses. For fast people they have fast horses; for slow people, they have slow horses. And for people who don't know how to ride at all, they have horses that have never been ridden before!

I don't know what your taste is, but when it comes to the Lord's work, there is a horse you can ride. Best of all, whatever the form your ministry takes, be it structured or informal, whether in the church or out in the marketplace, it is a way to help a few daring ones get involved in making disciples. When the Great Commission is seen as a life-style, nothing becomes insignificant, and everything that happens helps us know more of the grace of God.

Never Stop Learning

Whatever has been experienced thus far, there is more to learn. Keeping disciples pressing on is not easy. Anyone trying to help others is sure to face frustration. As I heard a colleague say, "Ministry would be easy, if it were not for people." Innumerable things can happen to sidetrack the best of intentions, and unless these matters are faced realistically, young disciples can easily become defeated. Persist in checking up. Ask how they are coming along. Sharing out of your experiences may encourage greater openness, as well as show your own accountability.

Probably the most deceiving problems in human relations come out when the ego is offended, giving rise to various expressions of self-centeredness, like pride or bitterness. Where these fleshly traits are recognized, they must be brought to the cross. Rebuke will not be resented when given in love, especially if we build self-esteem in them through consistent commendation of every evidence of progress in their developing priesthood.

Giving this kind of leadership puts us on the spot. Perhaps that is why we have such difficulty equipping disciples, for it means that we must be prepared to have them follow us, even as we follow the Lord (1 Cor. 11:1).

It makes us vulnerable, of course. Persons whom we let into the inner workings of our lives will surely see our shortcomings and failures. But let them also see a readiness to confess our sins when we understand the error of our ways. Let them hear us apologize to those we have wronged. Weaknesses need not impair discipleship when there is transparent sincerity to follow Christ. An honest exposure may tarnish our halo, but in seeing our humanness, others may more easily identify with our precepts. Furthermore, if we learn from our failures, as abundant as they are, there is no end to the lessons we'll derive.

Though we are witnesses, let us *make clear that Christ is the authority, not ourselves*. Avoid any authoritarian role of a master guru. Jesus alone commands. In subjection to Him, discipler and disciple together learn at His feet.

Leave With a Vision

Aided by your example, those persons close to you will begin to realize how Christ has ordered your steps. Now you can specifically share your philosophy of ministry with them. They will be able to understand, for in some measure they will have seen its interpretation in your investment in them.[22]

You can dream together about their place in the harvest and how God will use their unique personalities and gifts in ways far beyond your own. As they get their vision focused, encourage them to set some goals for the future as to where they would like to be ten, twenty, thirty years hence. With these projections in view, the next step is to help them map out plans to achieve their aims. It is in these hours of dreaming that a long-term strategy of discipling really takes shape.

The time will come, as with all physical relationships, when it will be necessary to withdraw from an active role in their lives. Bonds of love, though, will remain and perhaps even deepen. As they move on, others will take their place, and the process begins again. With each succeeding spiritual generation, anticipation of the harvest grows, looking joyously to the day when disciples will be made of all nations, and there will be a reunion in the sky.

A World Christian

My mother made the worldwide scope of Christianity real to me. She was truly a world Christian, living in expectation of the coming Kingdom.[23]

---

22. I cannot restrain the conviction that the reason so much confusion surrounds the Great Commission as commonly preached in the church is just that: It is preached, but not demonstrated. I have come to the conclusion that without the example, making disciples remains little more than a theory.

23. *World Christian* was a term often used by the late Dr. Herbert Kane. In his book *The Christian World Mission Today and Tomorrow* (Grand Rapids, Mich.: Baker Book House, 1981), he defines such a person as "one who acknowledges the universal fatherhood of God and the universal lordship of Christ, one who recognizes the cosmopolitan composition of the Christian church and the prime importance of the

Once I remember she said that as a girl she wanted to be a foreign missionary. As it turned out, though, that was not the way God led, and her ministry largely unfolded in our modest home in Texas. By today's standards, we were poor, and there was never enough money to buy a new car or to travel far from the city where the three children were born.

But in our imaginations we learned to project our thoughts to the ends of the earth. Mom was vitally involved in the church missionary society. She was always talking about what the missionaries were doing around the world, and out of her meager resources, she gave much to their support. Before she died in the arms of my sister, one of the last things she said was, "Be sure my missionary pledge is paid up."

Something of her priorities rubbed off on her family, a realization that has grown in me as I have tried to understand how every believer can live in the spirit of the Great Commission mandate.

The Call to Prayer

I have also come to see that the greatest expression of this vision will be seen in our prayers. It is here, in communion with the Spirit of Christ, that we enter most deeply into that love which drove Him into the world and now constrains us to beseech " 'the Lord of the harvest . . . to send out workers into his harvest field' " (Matt. 9:38). Indeed, this was Christ's

---

Christian mission," and finally, "one who recognizes his own personal responsibility for all phases of the Christian world mission." He goes on to say that "a world Christian will seek to increase his knowledge of world affairs, broaden his views of the church, increase his understanding of the Christian mission, enlarge the people of his prayer life, go abroad if opportunity affords, change his lifestyle, and recognize his personal responsibility for world missions." (Taken from the chapter "Every Christian a World Christian," 57–69.) Characteristic of his life's passion, Dr. Kane's last book before his death was entitled, *Wanted: World Christians* (Grand Rapids, Mich.: Baker Book House, 1986).

first missionary command.[24] Whatever we do begins as we wait on our knees before the throne of grace.

Jesus calls His disciples to get priorities in order. To pray is to confess our own utter inability to do anything in our own strength. At the same time, it is an affirmation that God is able; nothing is too hard for Him. As He commands, so He provides.

How He expects us to entreat God for harvesters can be seen in His own prayers. In these conversations with the Father, the deepest concerns of our Lord's life find utterance. For this reason, I believe that the seventeenth chapter of John is the most profound insight we have into the mind of Christ, for it is His longest recorded discourse on prayer.

Have you noticed that most of the prayer concerns His disciples? After rejoicing in His relationship with the Father (John 17:1–5), He turns his attention to those men "given" to Him out of the world (John 17:6–10). He prays for their protection from the evil one (John 17:11–15); He prays that they might have His joy in doing the will of God (John 17:13); and as they are sent into the world on a mission like His own, He prays that they will be sanctified—completely set apart for God's purpose—even as He sanctifies Himself (John 17:17–19). Nothing must be allowed to distract them from the work to which they are called, for "through their message," the world will believe on Him (John 17:20 ff.).

Think of it! Though He knows that in a few hours they will forsake Him—even His chief spokesman will openly deny that He is a friend—yet His love will not let them go. He believes in them when they cannot believe in themselves.

This is the test of a true Shepherd, willing to give His life

---

24. In making this observation, David J. Hesselgrave also notes that Peter received his missionary vision on a housetop as he prayed (Acts 10:9 ff.), and Paul and Barnabas were sent out after a season of prayer and fasting in the church at Antioch (Acts 13:1–3). "Missions in Tomorrow's World," *Decision*, 32, no. 5 (May 1991), 14.

for the sheep. However weak and faltering His disciples may be, Jesus cherishes for them the highest that He knows in spiritual communion, that the love wherewith He is loved of the Father may be in them, and He in them (John 17:21–26). Nothing greater in experience can be conceived. That He could have such faith in these beaten, cowed, and bewildered disciples leaves us breathless in wonder.

Our Ultimate Ministry

Aren't you glad that He held on for them? For in a real sense He was also praying for us. Had it not been for His intercession on our behalf, we would not know Him today. That is why our most enduring ministry will not be in the time spent talking with disciples, but in our prayers for them.

Thank God for those faithful servants who held us up to the Father, when our faith was weak—moms and dads, wives, husbands, grandfathers and grandmothers, Sunday-school teachers, church elders and deacons, pastors, missionaries, faithful men and women who invested their lives—and their prayers—in us. In the same way, let us lift up those persons entrusted to our care. Even when it does not seem that they understand, still we can pray and believe God for them. He is faithful who has promised.

While the ultimate dimensions of the Kingdom are not yet visible, we know that our labor for the Lord is not in vain. The seed planted and nourished in the lives of disciples will someday bring forth a harvest. Our joy is in knowing that in generations unborn these prayers will still bear fruit, through them, in an ever-widening circle to the ends of the earth and to the coming of the Lord.

May I ask, Is this your life-style? If so, you walk on tiptoes, and live every day in the fulfillment of the Great Commission.

Part Three
The Promise

". . . Surely I am with you always, to the very end of the age."

Matt. 28:20

"You will receive power when the Holy Spirit comes on you; and you will be my witnesses. . . ."

Acts 1:8

The Indispensable Gift

The affirmation of Christ's all-encompassing authority erases any doubt about the triumph of His Kingdom; and the consequent command to disciple all nations settles the plan of action; but how can His faltering disciples succeed in their mission, once the Lord has returned to heaven? The answer comes in the concluding promise: " 'Surely I am with you always, to the very end of the age' " (Matt. 28:20).

Jesus knows that left to our own resources and ingenuity we are helpless. Only He who has all power is sufficient for the task. That is why He assures the disciples of His continuing presence, a truth earlier enunciated in His teaching on the Holy Spirit (John 14:14–20, 26; 15:26; 16:7, 12–16).

Luke's rendering of the Great Commission brings out this promise even more explicitly. " 'I am going to send you what my Father has promised . . . , ' " Jesus says (Luke 24:49). " '. . . Do not leave Jerusalem, but wait for the gift my Father promised, which you have heard me speak about. For John baptized with water, but in a few days you will be baptized with the Holy Spirit' " (Acts 1:4, 5). " '. . . Stay in the city until you have been clothed with power from on high' " (Luke 24:49). " 'You will receive power when the Holy Spirit comes on you; and you will be my witnesses . . .' " (Acts 1:8).

John underscores the same promise in his account of Christ sending His disciples into the world on a mission like His own (John 20:21). In anticipation of the Pentecostal outpouring, "he breathed on them, and said, 'Receive the Holy Spirit' " (John 20:22).[1]

Strangely, though, this indispensable provision may be overlooked. I am reminded of a British pastor who was quizzing his class on the Apostles' Creed. Each boy was to repeat one phrase of the creed. The first began, "I believe in God, the Father Almighty, maker of heaven and earth."

The second boy said, "I believe in Jesus Christ, His only Son, our Lord."

The recitation continued until it came to one spot. The minister looked up from his notes to see what caused the silence. One of the scholars said, "I'm sorry, sir, but the boy who believed in the Holy Spirit is absent today."

Many people, I am afraid, are absent when it comes to appropriating the promised gift of the Spirit. Whether through ignorance, misunderstanding, lack of faith, or something else, they never seem to tarry until endued with power from on high.

---

1. Jesus' word here, "breathed," is the same word used in the Greek Septuagint for the Hebrew term in Gen. 2:7, when God "breathed" into the creature He had made "the breath of life, and the man became a living being." Just as the divine breath of the Holy Spirit gave life to our forebears, so the Spirit of Christ imparts His life into His disciples, a power they were soon to experience in greater measure. In this passage, Jesus also speaks of the disciples' forgiving sin in others, an authority He exercised but that in the hands of the disciples can only be understood in conjunction with the Spirit's direction. Note the succession in the text. The movement begins with God the Father, proceeds through the Son, and is carried forward by the Spirit given by Christ. The authority to forgive or to retain sins is in the Spirit, who makes clear the work of Jesus proclaimed by the disciple. The gospel calls men and women to decision, and on the basis of that choice sins are remitted or retained. As G. Campbell Morgan states in *The Missionary Manifest*, "Words of absolution or sentence of retention can only be uttered, therefore, upon the fulfillment of the conditions declared by Christ himself" (Grand Rapids, Mich.: Baker Book House, 1970, first published 1909), 121. For a full discussion of this point, *see* 110–134.

Creative Power

God acts as the Father in administration; He is seen as the Son in revelation; but He moves as the Spirit in operation.[2] Though the three Persons of the Godhead are equal in glory and superiority, when the function of power becomes prominent, the activity of the third member of the Holy Trinity comes to the fore.[3]

We are introduced to Him in the first chapter of the Book of Genesis, when it says, ". . . The Spirit of God was hovering over the waters" (Gen. 1:2). He was the divine energy bringing into existence and ordering the cosmos as the Father commanded (cf. Job 26:13). By the same mighty power, God still upholds that which He has made (Ps. 104:30; Isa. 40:12), and apart from the Spirit's constant renewing, the universe and all its life systems would revert to nothingness.

The creative function of the Holy Spirit received particular attention when God made man in His own likeness (Gen. 1:26).[4] We are told that He "breathed into his nostrils the

2. This analogy oversimplifies the provinces of action within the Trinity, of course. Any formulation of the triune nature of God proves inadequate, for the very reason that human intelligence cannot fathom the divine mind. How three uncreated Persons can function in one essence is a mystery. Yet only by the Trinity can the personality of God be understood. For a discussion of this mystery, *see* R. C. Sproul, *The Mystery of the Holy Spirit* (Wheaton, Ill.: Tyndale House, 1990), 33–74.

3. There is no want of good material on this subject. Among the more popular introductions are the books of Billy Graham, *The Holy Spirit* (Waco, Tex.: Word, 1978); James Elder Cumming, *A Handbook on the Holy Spirit* (Minneapolis: Dimension Books, 1977, 1965); J. T. Seamonds, *On Tiptoe With Love* (Kansas City: Beacon Hill Press, 1971); J. I. Packer, *Keep In Step With the Spirit* (Old Tappan, N. J.: Fleming H. Revell Co., 1984); and Martin Lloyd Jones, *Joy Unspeakable* (Wheaton, Ill.: Harold Shaw Publishers, 1984).

4. A veiled reference to the Trinity may be seen in the deliberative council within the Godhead respecting the decision: " 'Let us make man in our image . . .' " (Gen. 1:26). "Us" indicates more than one (also in Gen. 3:22; 11:6, 7). Further strengthening this reference to the Trinity is the plural word for "God," *Elohim*, in Genesis 1:1. There is the passage, too, in Isa. 48:16 which speaks of a grouping of the persons of the Trinity. Though the concept of a plurality of persons within the being

breath of life" (Gen. 2:7). The word here for "breath" is the root for the word *Spirit*. Literally it means that God spiritualized the creature He formed from "the dust of the ground," and thereby "man became a living being" (Gen. 2:7). Thus Job testified, " 'The Spirit of God has made me; the breath of the Almighty gives me life' " (Job 33:4). Only through the interposition of the Spirit do we live and move and have our being in God.

Recreated in Christ

Tragically, however, God's purpose in making a people for His glory—to live in communion with Him—was lost because of sin. Though His Spirit still sought to bring a fallen race to God (Gen. 6:3; cf. Ps. 139:7), the inner presence of the Spirit was withdrawn, leaving our forebears not only depraved, but deprived of the means of divine fellowship. We all turned to our own way, vainly existing "without hope and without God in the world" (Eph. 2:12; cf. Gen. 3:8–24; Ps. 58:3; Rom. 3:23).

That is why, even to begin to live as God designed, we must be "born again"—"born of the Spirit" (John 3:3, 7, 8). " 'I tell you the truth,' " Jesus said, " 'no one can enter the kingdom of God unless he is born of water and the Spirit. Flesh gives birth to flesh, but the Spirit gives birth to spirit' " (John 3:5, 6; cf. 6:63; Rom. 8:11; 2 Cor. 3:6; 1 Pet. 3:18). This does not mean that God destroys our humanity. Rather He takes our corrupted natures and, through the regenerating ministry of the Holy Spirit, redirects our lives according to His

---

of one God emerges early in the Old Testament, the emphasis is more upon the unity of His nature, perhaps in consideration that the limited understanding of the people and the temptation to idolatry, might lead them to see the persons of the Godhead as three distinct Gods.

created purpose (John 1:12; 2 Cor. 5:17; Titus 3:5; cf. Eze. 36:26).

Once we have been transformed by His power, the Spirit continues to nourish and strengthen us as growing children of God. His renewing work is likened to a spring of " 'living water' . . . 'welling up to eternal life' " within us (John 7:38; 4:14). He witnesses with our spirits that we belong to God (Rom. 8:14; Gal. 4:6; 1 John 3:24; 4:13). He convicts us of sin (John 16:8–11). He helps us pray, interpreting the groanings of our hearts to the Father (Rom. 8:26, 27; cf. Eph. 6:18). He enables us to worship (John 4:24). He guides into truth, ever teaching us more of our Lord (John 14:26; 16:13; 1 John 2:7; cf. Neh. 9:20; Ps. 143:10).

As we obey His leading, confessing our sin when convicted, we are made clean "by the truth," and walk in fellowship with God (John 17:17; cf. 15:3; Eph. 5:26; 1 John 1:7, 9). The fruits of the Spirit, character traits so beautifully portrayed in Christ—"love, joy, peace, patience, kindness, goodness, faithfulness, gentleness and self-control"— begin to flow from our lives (Gal. 5:22, 23; cf. Phil. 1:11; Col. 1:10; Eph. 5:9; John 15:5). With our "minds set on what the Spirit desires," we are progressively changed into the character of Jesus "with ever-increasing glory" (Rom. 8:5; 2 Cor. 3:18). Finally, on the resurrection morning, our very mortal bodies will be changed into the likeness of our Lord's glorified form (Rom. 8:11; 1 Cor. 15:44, 49; Phil. 3:21). From beginning to end, partaking of the saving life of Christ is the Spirit's work.

Preparing Redemption

As you would expect, too, it was the same Person of the Trinity who prepared the way for the Savior's coming into the world. In the Old Testament few people knew the Spirit's power, but from time to time He would come upon selected persons and equip them to perform a service in God's unfolding plan of salvation.

We are told, for example, that the Spirit of God was with Joseph in Egypt (Gen. 41:38). He qualified Moses to lead the children of Israel, just as He prepared the seventy elders who assisted Him (Num. 11:17, 25, 26, 29). When it came time to build the tabernacle, a pattern of redemption to be consummated in Christ, the Spirit filled Bezalel and Oholiab with skill and knowledge for the task (Ex. 31:2, 3, 6; 35:30, 31, 34). In the same way, the Spirit qualified those appointed to make the robes for Aaron and his priestly sons (Ex. 28:3, 4).[5]

All through the history of Israel the divine Spirit can be seen at work making a nation to accomplish His purpose (Hag. 2:5). He raised up judges for His people (Num. 27:18; Deut. 34:19; Judges 3:10; 6:34; 11:29; 13:25; 14:6, 19; 15:14) and later the kings (1 Sam. 10:6; 11:6; 16:13; 2 Sam. 23:1, 2). Tragically, these leaders too often betrayed their trust, and the Spirit departed from them.[6] But insofar as they fulfilled God's mission in the world, it was the third Person of the Holy Trinity who qualified them for the task.

At times the Spirit came upon prophets and inspired them

5. No priest in the Old Testament could come before the altar without this proper clothing. Interestingly, the Hebrew word for "coat" has the root meaning "to cover" or "to hide." It is the same word used in Genesis 3:21, when it says that God made coats of skin to cover Adam and Eve. The robe worn by the priests was in this sense a way of showing that they ministered, not in their own righteousness, but in the covering of the blameless Lamb of God and High Priest of heaven. For amplification of this meaning, *see* my book, *Written in Blood* (Old Tappan, N. J.: Fleming H. Revell Co., 1972), 40–42. A beautiful study of the garments worn by the priests as related to Christ is by C. W. Slemming, *These Are the Garments*, rev. ed. (Chicago: Moody Press, 1955).

6. Saul is a notable example (1 Sam. 16:14). Samson is another (Judges 15:14; cf. 16:20). Because of their sin, God no longer could use them. They tried to do the same old thing, but the Spirit was not in it. The danger of this happening can be seen in the prayer of David after he had committed sin with Bathsheba. Knowing the consequences of his act, he earnestly besought the Lord that the Spirit would not be taken from him (Ps. 51:11). Nothing is more futile than trying to carry on God's work in the energy of the flesh.

to communicate a message of the Lord (cf. 1 Sam. 19:20, 23; 2 Sam. 23:1, 2; Neh. 9:20, 30; Eze. 11:5; Mic. 3:8; Zech. 7:12). Our whole confidence in what they said and later wrote in the Scriptures rests upon the fact that they were borne along by the Spirit of God (2 Pet. 1:21; cf. Matt. 22:43; Mark 12:36; Acts 1:16; 28:25; 2 Tim. 3:16).

Under His inspiration a day was envisioned when God's plan of redemption would consummate in the coming of Messiah. A virgin would conceive, and she would bear a son, who would be called Immanuel—"God with us" (Isa. 7:14; Matt. 1:23). Upon this Branch growing out of the root of David, the Spirit of the Lord would rest without measure (Isa. 11:1, 2), and through Him a new age would dawn when the Spirit would be poured out upon all flesh (Isa. 32:15; cf. Joel 2:28–32; Hag. 2:4–7; Zech. 12:10; 14:8).

Ministry of the Son

Just as foretold, in the fullness of time, He who had been working from the beginning to effect God's purpose now planted the seed of the Father in the womb of the virgin so that she conceived and brought forth into human experience the only begotten Son of God (Matt. 1:18, 20; Luke 1:35).[7] Thereafter the Spirit directs His incarnate life, not in a limited degree or for a special time, as His predecessors in Israel, but in full measure and permanent possession.[8]

The fullness of the Spirit receives particular attention as

---

7. In other respects the physical birth of Christ was not unlike our own. What the Scripture makes clear is that His conception was different. That is where life begins. Pro-choice advocates in the abortion debate should take note.

8. As a perfect man, of course, Jesus had a spirit of His own, like anyone else (Mark 2:8; John 11:33; 13:21; 19:30; Matt. 27:50; cf. Eccl. 12:7). How His spiritual nature was fused with the Holy Spirit lies within the mystery of His human and divine personality. We know that He felt the same natural sensibilities as we do, but His human spirit yielded fully to the Spirit of God.

Jesus begins His public ministry (Luke 4:1, 14, 15; Mark 1:12). John the Baptist's announcement that He will baptize with " 'the Holy Spirit and with fire' " further uncovers the spiritual nature of His mission (Matt. 3:11; Mark 1:8; Luke 3:16). Later, explaining why Christ is preeminent in all that He does, John added: " 'For the one whom God has sent speaks the words of God; for God gives the Spirit without limit' " (John 3:34; cf. Luke 10:21). To dramatize His unique relationship with the Godhead, at the river Jordan the Spirit was seen descending upon the Master like a dove, and a voice spoke from heaven, confirming the Father's pleasure in the Son (Matt. 3:13–17; Mark 1:9–11; Luke 3:21–23; cf. John 1:32–34).

Lest this divine endorsement for His mission be missed, upon His first invitation to speak at His home synagogue at Nazareth, Jesus stood up and read from the scroll of Isaiah: " 'The Spirit of the Lord is on me, because he has anointed me to preach good news to the poor. He has sent me to proclaim freedom for the prisoners and recovery of sight for the blind, to release the oppressed, to proclaim the year of the Lord's favor' " (Luke 4:18, 19; cf. Isa. 61:1, 2). Having read the lesson, He rolled up the parchment, gave it back to the attendant, then sat down and announced to the startled congregation, " 'Today this Scripture is fulfilled in your hearing' " (Luke 4:21).

The Spirit's power through the works of Christ displayed His authority over the demonic structure of this world and thereby evidenced the coming of the Kingdom of God (Matt. 12:27, 28). Those who rejected the claims of Christ, of course, were unwilling to accept this conclusion. To do so would require a recognition of His messianic mission. So they took the other option and accused Him of being in league with the devil. Whereupon Jesus warned the unbelieving Jews that they were in danger of committing an unpardonable sin—they were blaspheming the Holy Spirit (Matt. 12:31, 32; Mark 3:28, 29; cf. Luke 11:14–26).[9]

Clearly the Spirit was ever present in Christ to make His life a revelation of God. Whatever He said and did was a demonstration of this mission. Finally, by "the eternal Spirit," He "offered himself unblemished to God" as our atoning sacrifice (Heb. 9:14); then through the same instrumentality, He was raised from the dead (Rom. 8:11; cf. 1:4).

Continuing Christ's Work

As the Spirit fulfilled God's saving Word in Christ, so also He would enable His disciples to make known the good news of His completed work, to the ends of the earth (Acts 1:8). Through His power, they would be equipped to do the very works of their Lord, and even "greater things than these" (John 14:22). Jesus does not elaborate on these "greater" deeds, but His promise would seem to relate to the multiplication of disciples according to the Great Commission mandate.[10]

---

9. Jesus does not say here that the Pharisees were beyond redemption, but that by their hostile attitude they reflected a condition that, unless reversed, would bring final separation from God's mercy. To scorn Christ is to reject the only way of salvation and hence to be in a state of unforgiveness. If one persists in this rejection, the state of judgment becomes permanent—one is guilty of an eternal sin.

10. A greater work can be seen in the ensuing ministry of those first believers in the Acts of the Apostles. Not only is there greater geographic expansion of the church, but also the numerical increase of believers is no less remarkable. When Christ returned to heaven, we are told there were scarcely more than five hundred believers, and these were primarily located within the confines of Israel (1 Cor. 15:6). But when the Spirit came upon the disciples at Pentecost, that one day about three thousand were converted, and among them were pilgrims from at least fifteen other language groups (Acts 2:9–11). Every day thereafter others were added to the church as they were saved (Acts 2:41, 47), and Christians began to witness across the earth. Indeed, the Book of Acts really has no conclusion, for we are still living in this promise of "greater things," and it will not end until the Great Commission is fulfilled.

They are under no illusion that the work will be easy. Indeed, the disciples can expect the same hatred from the world as was directed against their Lord (John 15:18–27). But when they were under duress, Jesus told them not to worry, for the Spirit would give them utterance to speak (Matt. 10:16–23; Mark 13:11; Luke 12:12). He would lift up the Son, and as men and women see His glory, they will be convicted of their "guilt in regard to sin and righteousness and judgment" (John 16:8–11).[11]

What a load this takes off our shoulders. It is not our responsibility to convince anyone of the truth. That is the Spirit's work. All we can do is witness to the gospel and leave the matter of persuasion to God. The Spirit will apply the message and draw broken and contrite hearts to the Savior.[12]

Another Counselor

As His days on earth drew to a close, Jesus was particularly concerned that His disciples understand how He would carry on His ministry through them by the Holy Spirit.[13] The teaching comes out most beautifully on the eve of His crucifixion,

---

11. Under conviction of the Spirit, persons are brought to see their unbelief in Christ, which is the epitome of sin. In so doing, they are made to recognize in Christ's completed work at Calvary the only way one can appear righteous before a holy God. Moreover, the world's standard of truth is seen to be utterly in error. Jesus, rejected by the world, is exalted in heaven; whereas the prince of this world, Satan, now stands condemned.

12. Much superficiality in present-day evangelism efforts could be avoided if this truth were observed. All too easily we try to induce human response to the gospel through behavioral and psychological manipulation. Not only do such practices produce stillborn converts, but they cheapen the witness of the church in the world.

13. For a good treatment of Jesus' teaching on the Spirit, *see* Louis Burton Crane, *The Teaching of Jesus Concerning the Holy Spirit* (New York: American Tract Society, 1905); J. Ritchie Smith, *The Holy Spirit in the Gospels* (New York: Macmillan, 1926); and Henry Barclay Swete, *The Holy Spirit in the New Testament* (Grand Rapids, Mich.: Baker Book House, 1976).

while they were together in the upper room, after the Pascal supper (John 14:1—16:33). Knowing that soon He must go, Jesus told the disciples that He would not leave them orphans. When He returned to heaven, He would ask the Father to give them "another Counselor" to take His place, even "the Spirit of truth" (John 14:16, 17).

No theory, no makeshift substitute. The reference is to a real Person, like Himself; "another" to stand by their sides— one who would be with them in spiritual reality just as their Master had been with them in His physical presence.[14] Heretofore Jesus had been their counselor and teacher, but now the Spirit would guide them into all truth (John 14:26; 16:13); He would answer their questions (John 16:23); He would show them the future (John 16:13); He would enable them to speak to God in the name of their Lord (John 14:12, 13; 16:23, 24). In short, He would glorify Christ in the lives of His disciples (John 15:26; 16:14–16).

Actually their relationship to Jesus through the Spirit was to be more fulfilling than anything experienced before. In the flesh Jesus was limited to one body and one place; He could not be with His disciples all the time. With those physical barriers removed, however, through the Spirit, the disciples could live continually in the presence of their Lord. That is why He could say, " 'I am with you always, to the very end of the age' " (Matt. 28:20; cf. John 14:16).

This is the promise in which the Great Commission lives and has its being—the means by which disciples go forth to

---

14. The word "another" here is not the term used to compare two objects different in quality; rather this is a term used to compare two different persons or objects that have the same essential quality. While the word recognizes the difference between the second and third members of the Trinity, in quality of life—in holiness, in love, in truth, in power—the incarnate Word and the invisible Spirit are the same. G. Campbell Morgan discusses this distinction in *The Teaching of Christ* (New York: Fleming H. Revell Co., 1913), 65.

disciple the nations. Jesus is with us, not as a distant observer, but as a present associate. Note, too, that it is not a promise obtained when we get to heaven, but a fellowship to be experienced now as we obey His command.

Until Jesus had finished His work on earth and was exalted at the right hand of God, the promise could not be realized (John 7:39; Acts 2:33). But after Jesus returned to take His place of supremacy at the heavenly throne, the Spirit could be released in power upon the expectant church; not for a few years, but for an age; not on a few choice individuals, but on all who would receive Him.

The Pentecostal Outpouring

It is easy to see why Jesus told His disciples to tarry until this power was experienced (Luke 24:49; Acts 1:5, 8). How else could they ever do His work? Their enthroned Lord needed to become a living reality in their ministry. "The very Spirit of God's own Son, as he had lived and loved, had obeyed and died," had "to become their personal life."[15] Unless they were enthralled by His Presence, His mission would never captivate their souls.

The awaited empowerment begins to unfold at Pentecost.[16] As the disciples were assembled at Jerusalem in prayer, suddenly a sound like the blowing of a violent wind came from heaven and filled the house where they were sitting (Acts 2:2). The wind, symbolizing the strength of the Spirit, came first to the believing fellowship, from whence it would sweep across the earth with life-giving power. Then "they saw what

---

15. Andrew Murray, *The Spirit of Christ* (London: Nesbet and Co., 1880), 149.
16. Among the many studies on this subject, probably the most complete in reference to the Great Commission is Henry Boer's work, *Pentecost and Mission* (Grand Rapids, Mich.: Wm. B. Eerdmans, 1961).

seemed to be tongues of fire that separated and came to rest on each of them" (Acts 2:3). The distribution of the sacred fire pointed to the truth that the Spirit had come to dwell with all the members of the church. Descriptive, too, of their witness-bearing function, they "began to speak in other tongues as the Spirit enabled them" (Acts 2:4).

The enduring miracle on this day, however, was not in the signs dramatizing the event,[17] but rather in the way the disciples were "filled with the Holy Spirit" (Acts 2:4), an experience repeatedly underscored in the ensuing account of the apostolic church.[18] Jesus as an external Presence now reigned as Sovereign in their hearts. The gospel became life and power within them.

The full significance of this heavenly enducment becomes increasingly apparent as we move through the Book of Acts. What joyous assurance emboldens the disciples in their witness! A purity of intention drives them. Their hearts overflow in praise to God. When beaten and stoned, they pray for their tormentors. Something about them was different. "Look how

---

17. The wind and the fire do not reappear in subsequent visitations of the Spirit in the Acts of the Apostles, and tongues are only noted twice (Acts 10:46; 19:6). Tongues are mentioned by Paul when he speaks of spiritual gifts in his letter to the Corinthian church, but nowhere does he indicate that the gift is any evidence of divine favor. In fact, most of the teaching in regard to tongues cautions against an undue attention to them (1 Cor. 12:1–31; 13:1; 14:1–40; cf. Rom. 12:6–8; Eph. 4:8).
18. Noted in Acts 4:8, 31; 6:3, 5; 7:55; 9:17; 11:24; 13:9, 52; cf. Luke 1:15, 41, 67; 4:1. The figure conveys the idea of a personality being pervaded by the Spirit's power and influence. In some instances the text underscores an act of being filled; in other usages the emphasis is upon acting in the fullness of the Spirit. That the Spirit-filled life was understood as the norm of Christian experience is seen in Eph. 5:18, where Paul exhorts the saints to be constantly filled with the Spirit. The tenses here underscore a moment-by-moment abiding in Christ. Other descriptions of the Spirit's personal bestowal are mentioned in the Acts about twenty-five times, with words like *receive, give, fall, pour out, baptize, anoint,* or *come;* and these terms sometimes relate to an infilling. Each instance needs to be interpreted in its own context.

they love each other," one observer noted.[19] There was a
sparkle in their eyes, a deep serenity in their souls. By watch-
ing them closely, even their antagonists could tell that they
"had been with Jesus" (Acts 4:13).

Needless to say, not every Christian lived in the fullness of
the Spirit. Accounts of the early church reflect ample problems with strife and pettiness among believers. But where
these conditions existed, the New Testament made abundantly clear that carnal saints were living below the expectations of their Lord.

Receiving the Promise

Pentecost marked the beginning of an era that would continue
until Spirit-empowered witnesses bear the gospel to the ends
of the earth. To be sure, as a historical event, the outpouring
on that day can never be repeated—it is an accomplished fact;
but the spiritual enduement it gave to the church continues
for all generations. Nothing about the power from on high is
restricted to the apostolic church. As Peter proclaimed, " 'The
promise is for you and your children and for all who are far
off—for all whom the Lord our God will call' " (Acts 2:39).

And why should any believer not have the blessing? " 'Everyone who asks, receives . . . , " Jesus said (Luke 11:10).
Then, to underscore this truth, He reminded His disciples
that if an earthly father, being evil, knows how to give good
gifts to his children, " '. . . how much more will your Father
in heaven give the Holy Spirit to those who ask Him!' "
(Luke 11:13).

Obviously, though, receiving the Spirit in fullness requires
that our hearts be empty of that which hinders His possession.

19. Quoted by Tertullian, *Apology* 39, 40, in Eberhard Arnold, ed., *The Early Christians* (Grand Rapids, Mich.: Baker Book House, 1979), 112.

Where there is known sin, it must be confessed and our characters conformed to all that we know of Christ. He must be Lord of our lives. Not that we can have all of Him, of course. No human can ever contain the infinite personality of God. But He wants all of us.

As we learn more of Him through obedience, so also our capacity to experience His life will enlarge. There is never a foreclosure on growth in grace and knowledge. His presence is fresh every morning. Special anointings of the Spirit will be needed as new demands of ministry require greater sensitivity and strength. Yet however difficult the task, we can rest on the promise that Jesus is with us, never to leave, never to forsake His own.

How we describe this abiding may differ, depending upon theological presuppositions.[20] *What matters is not the definition, but the reality of the ever-present Savior and Lord in our lives.*

An Example

Many people engaged in the work of Christ may not easily embrace this promise. Dwight L. Moody was such a person. Though very energetic, for years he labored largely in the energy of the flesh.

Sensing the problem, two dear ladies, burdened for his ministry, mentioned that they were praying for Him. Mr. Moody wanted to know why they were praying for Him rather

---

20. Some persons, for example, may equate the Pentecostal infilling with true conversion. Others look upon it as a spiritual event after regeneration. That the experience is variously identified in Scripture adds to the difficulty. Perhaps it may be agreed that everyone receives the Spirit when saved, though the fullness of the Spirit may not be realized until later or the conditions maintained. However interpreted, it is clear that the Spirit must have undisputed reign in the heart. To see how people may know the same reality in different ways, read V. Raymond Edman, *They Found the Secret* (Grand Rapids, Mich.: Zondervan, 1984).

than the unsaved. "Oh," they said, "We are praying that you will get the power."[21] The evangelist did not understand what they meant and at first was rather irritated by their concern. But as time went on, he asked them to tell Him more about the Spirit, and he joined them in prayer.

Not long after this, one day while walking down Wall Street, in New York City, their prayers were answered. The Spirit came upon Him with such force that he had to ask God to stay His hand, because he could hold no more. From that time on, his life and work reflected a new spiritual depth and power.

As with others who have known such a definite renewing of the heart, the power of the Spirit became a growing emphasis in Moody's ministry, particularly when he addressed potential church leaders. Being a very practical-minded man, he could not understand why some people would obscure this essential truth by academic disputation on peripheral matters. "Oh, why will they split hairs?" he said one day to Dr. R. A. Torrey, after a frustrating discussion with some teachers. "Why don't they see that this is just the one thing that they themselves need?"[22]

Dr. Torrey recalls an occasion in the summer of 1894, which illustrates Mr. Moody's feeling. It was the closing day of the Northfield Conference, where students had gathered from a number of eastern colleges. Torrey, at Moody's request, had preached that morning on the baptism of the Holy Spirit. When he finished, at noon, he told the students that Moody had invited them "to go up on the mountain at three o'clock to pray for the power of the Holy Spirit." But

---

21. Taken from the account of R. A. Torrey, a close associate of Moody and in many ways his successor, in *Why God Used D. Moody* (Chicago: Moody Bible Institute, 1923), 56. For Moody's own account of the Spirit's ministry, *see* his *Secret Power, or the Secret of Success in Christian Life and Work* (New York: Fleming H. Revell Co., 1881).
22. Torrey, *Why God Used D. Moody*, 60.

he said, "Some of you cannot wait those hours. You do not need to wait. Go to your rooms; go out into the woods; go anywhere you can get alone with God and have the matter out."[23]

At three o'clock the more than four hundred students assembled and went up the mountain. After a while, Mr. Moody said: "I don't think we need to go any further; let us sit down here."[24] So they sat down on the ground and on logs under the trees.

"Have any of you anything to say?" he asked. Many of the students arose, one after another, to say that they could not wait, and since the morning service they had been alone with God, and could affirm that they had received the promised enduement of the Spirit.

When their testimonies were finished, Mr. Moody said: "Young men, I can't see any reason why we shouldn't kneel down here right now and ask God that the Holy Ghost may fall on us just as definitely as he fell upon the apostles on the Day of Pentecost. Let us pray."[25]

As they had gone up the mountain that day heavy clouds had been gathering. Dr. Torrey says:

> Just as we began to pray those clouds broke and the raindrops began to fall through the overhanging pines. But there was another cloud that had been gathering over Northfield, a cloud big with the mercy and grace and power of God; and as we began to pray our prayers seemed to pierce that cloud and the Holy Ghost fell upon us.[26]

---

23. Ibid., 61.
24. Ibid., 62.
25. Ibid., 62.
26. Ibid., 62, 63.

That is what all of us need—a heavenly anointing of the Spirit of Christ. Thanks be to God, if His presence is not a reality in our lives, we do not have to wait. The Comforter has come; He is here now. And all who surrender to Him as Lord will abide in the promise of the Great Commission.

" 'Love the Lord your God with all your heart and with all your soul and with all your mind. . . . Love your neighbor as yourself.' All the Law and the Prophets hang on these two commandments."

Matt. 22:37, 39, 40

"Simon son of John, do you love me?"

John 21:17

Epilogue

Conclusion of the Matter

The question remains: What are we going to do about the Great Commission? Christ's affirmation, mandate, and promise all call for a response. The issues that are addressed do not permit us the luxury of indifference. We must decide.

Too easily this kind of study becomes an academic exercise. More intellectual stimulation may be helpful, of course, but that is not where the matter is settled. After thirty-five years of teaching in graduate schools, I am of the conviction that the reason so much confusion attends the mission of the church lies, not with our heads, but with our hearts. It comes down finally to love.

Jesus made this abundantly clear when He said: " ' "Love the Lord your God with all your heart and with all your soul and with all your mind." This is the first and greatest commandment. And the second is like it: "Love your neighbor as yourself." All the Law and the Prophets hang on these two commandments' " (Matt. 22:37–40; Mark 12:28–33; cf. Matt. 5:43–48; Luke 6:27–36; 10:27; Deut. 6:5; Lev. 19:18). Out of this Great Commandment flows the Great Commission.

Where such love motivates our labor, the effort cannot be in vain; but when it is not the heartbeat of our work, whatever we do will be wasted energy (1 Cor. 13:1–13). In its larger context, then, everything about our lives turns on love.

Confronting the Question

This truth runs through Scripture, but it is focused no where more personally by Jesus than in a confrontation with Peter after the resurrection (John 21:1–23). Some of the disciples had been fishing all night on the sea of Tiberias and had caught nothing. As the dawn began to break, Jesus appeared on the shore, though they did not recognize Him in the mist. Showing an interest in their occupation, He asked about their catch. When they confessed their failure, He told them to cast their net on the right side of the boat. Instinctively, they followed His directions, and almost immediately their nets filled with fish.

The experience recalls an incident a few years before, when four of these same disciples, after a night of fishing without success, were told by Jesus to launch out into deeper waters and let down their nets. When they obeyed, the catch of fish was so great that the boat began to sink, and they had to call for help. Afterward, Jesus entreated them to follow Him, and He would make them fishers of men (Matt. 4:18–22; Mark 1:16–20; Luke 5:1–11).

As the disciples struggled to bring in the nets, the similarity with the other experience could not be mistaken, and John exclaimed: " 'It is the Lord!' " (John 21:7). At this, Peter, unable to restrain his excitement, dove into the water and swam ashore.

When the disciples got their boat to land, Jesus had a fire kindled and some fish frying over it. He asked them to bring over some of their fish and join Him for breakfast.

When they had finished eating, Jesus asked Peter, ". . .'Simon son of John, do you truly love me more than these?'. . ." After a strong affirmative response, the big fisherman was told: ". . .'Feed my lambs' " (John 21:15).

Not content to leave the issue, however, Jesus asked again, " 'Simon son of John, do you truly love me?'. . ." Receiving the same answer, Jesus made a similar application (John 21:16). Then, without further comment, He quickly came back to the decisive question, ". . .'Simon son of John, do you love me?'. . ." (John 21:17).

Grieved that Jesus would interrogate him about this three times, Peter adamantly affirmed: ". . .'Lord, you know all things; you know that I love you'. . . ." Whereupon, after reemphasizing the necessity of feeding His sheep, Jesus told Peter what love would cost in obedience (John 21:17–22).

By focusing on this truth in the discourse, Jesus brought out the underlying question in Christian service. Though He spoke to Peter, His words were uttered in the hearing of the other disciples and could just as well be directed to everyone who would follow Him. You can hear Him call your name, as He asks, "Bill, Mary—Simon son of John, do you truly love me?"

Loving Jesus

Observe that *Jesus* is the object of love, not a creed, not a church, not a religion. Jesus asks, "Do you love *me?*"

He sets Himself before us as the way to know God. In His meeting with the disciples, following the last supper, remember how He told them in no uncertain terms that He was "the true way of life" (John 14:6).[1] A paraphrase of this statement might read, "I am the beginning, the middle, and the end of the ladder to heaven."[2] He has purchased our redemption in His own blood and freely offers every blessing of grace to all who come unto God through Him (Matt. 11:28, 29; cf. John 17:2).

" 'Simon, do you love me?' "

There was good reason to ask. Not long before, Peter had three times denied his Lord. The memory of that tragic fail-

---

1. Augustine's summation of this text, subordinating the last attributes to the first, is quoted in John Peter Lange, *Commentary on the Holy Scriptures, John,* trans. Philip Schaff (Grand Rapids, Mich.: Zondervan, n.d.), 437.
2. A rendering of Martin Luther, ibid.

ure was doubtless awakened by the thrice-repeated question, just as the fire must have reminded him of that night in the palace courtyard, when he swore that he was no friend of Jesus (Matt. 26:69–75; Mark 14:66–72; Luke 22:54–62; John 18:25–27).

Yes, Peter had repented and wept bitterly, but Jesus' question is not, "How much do you regret the past?" not, "How many tears have been shed?" but "Do you love *me?*" It is His preeminence in our hearts that makes the other expressions acceptable.

Or the words might be taken to mean, "Do you love me more than these things?"—more than the comforts of home, more than the acclaim of a good reputation, more even than the work you are doing for Him. Not that these other things are undeserving of love, but Jesus expects to be loved *more.* The giving of Himself for you precludes any rival to your devotion. You may not amount to much, but whatever you are, He wants all of it.

He Knows Our Heart

Interestingly, on the last occasion, when Peter affirmed his love, he added: ". . .'Lord, you know all things; you know that I love you' " (John 21:17). With his memory of past failure, he could not appeal to his record, but he could appeal to his Lord's understanding.

What a comfort to the soul! Jesus knows all about it. We don't have to explain our situation to Him. In His infinite knowledge, He interprets the thoughts and intents of the heart; He knows when we truly love Him.

I remember a time, years ago, when my son made this truth so real to me. It was a hot afternoon at the end of the harvest season, and I was out in the backyard, cleaning up my garden.

Jim, who was then no more than three or four years old, saw me working, and it occurred to him that I was thirsty. So he pulled a chair up to the kitchen sink, got a dirty glass, and filled it with water from the faucet. The next thing I knew, my name was being called. As I turned around, there was my son coming across the garden, holding that smudgy glass of warm water, saying, "Daddy, I thought you were thirsty, so I brought you a drink." And as he held up the glass, a smile stretched across his face from one ear to the other.

You might think, *Couldn't he do better than that?* Why, that was not cool water; it was not even pure water. And you would be right. But when you looked at his face, you would have had to say that was pure love. He was doing the best he knew to please his daddy.

In some similar way, that is how every disciple of Christ can love. Though we continually make errors in judgment and fall woefully short of our desire to be like Jesus, still in our hearts we can do the best we know to please Him. Can you appeal to His perfect understanding today, as did Peter, and say with all your soul, "Lord, You know all things; You know that I love You"?

Love Overflows

But the affirmation, sincere as it may be, needs expression in more than words. So each time Peter confesses his love, Jesus says, " 'Feed my sheep' " (John 21:15–17). He underscores that love overflows in ministry to the world.

Love for Christ, you see, cannot be self-contained, for it "comes from God" and thereby reflects something of His own nature (1 John 4:7, 8; cf. Rom. 5:5). It is the kind of love that would not let us go, even "while we were still sinners" (Rom. 5:8). Calvary is His witness.

As Jesus was hanging on the cross, recall how the worldings came by and mocked Him, saying, " 'He saved others, but he can't save himself'. . ." (Matt. 27:42; Mark 15:31; cf. Luke 23:35). The irony is that in their derision the scoffing crowd said the truth. Of course, He could not save Himself. That was the point. He had not come into the world to save Himself; He came to save us. He " 'came to seek and to save what was lost' " (Luke 19:10). " 'The Son of Man did not come to be served, but to serve, and to give his life as a ransom for many' " (Matt. 20:28; Mark 10:45).

Just as He was sent into the world, now He sends us (John 17:18; 20:21). "Christ's love compels us, because we are convinced that one died for all, and therefore all died. And he died for all, that those who live should no longer live for themselves but for him who died for them and was raised again" (2 Cor. 5:14, 15).

How It Works

His mission in the flesh now accomplished, Jesus tells His disciples to take care of those for whom He gave His life. People are likened to sheep that are lost without a shepherd. Left to themselves, there is no hope of recovery. Someone with the heart of Christ must go to them, tell them the gospel, and lead them to the fold of salvation. Then having come to Jesus, the sheep must be nurtured in His way; they need to be fed and clothed and protected from ravaging predators. It will require loving discipleship by committed servants. But with faithful shepherding, the sheep will grow up and someday begin to reproduce their kind.

There was a time when Peter was like a sheep, wandering aimlessly, without any direction in life. But now, through the miracle of divine grace, his nature had been so transformed that he was becoming like a shepherd.

In this ministry there is a place for us all. Our form of service will vary, depending upon gifts and callings, but God, who made us what we are, will use every disciple in some way to care for His sheep. And whatever is done truly for the love of Christ, even to " 'one of the least of these' " sheep, becomes an act of worship to the Lord (Matt. 25:40).

An incident in the life of Uncle John Vassar illustrates what I mean. A zealous soul winner for the Lord, he served as a colporteur for the American Tract Society. One day as he tried to share the gospel with a lady, she cut him off and refused to accept a tract. Not to be outdone, however, the old gentleman asked if he could sing her a song, and then proceeded to raise the verse:

> But drops of grief can ne'er repay
> The debt of love I owe:
> Here, Lord, I give myself away,
> 'Tis all that I can do.

As he finished singing the woman was utterly subdued and ultimately became a Christian. Giving her testimony in church, she said: "Ah, those drops of grief, those drops of grief—I couldn't get over them!"[3]

I am not suggesting that anyone follow Vassar's eccentric style. Methods of witnessing are variable and have no virtue in themselves. It's the love prompting them that makes all the difference. Would it be unfair to ask, "How is your love for Jesus finding practical expression in ministry to the sheep?"

---

3. Recounted in the story of Vassar's life, compiled by his nephew, T. E. Vassar, in *Uncle John Vassar; or, The Fight of Faith* (New York: The American Tract Society, 1879), 161.

Priority of the Unreached

As you ponder the question, consider carefully the priority of bringing the witness of Christ into the marketplace of today's unreached world—fields white unto harvest, yet where so few servants are laboring.

Do you realize that nearly half the peoples of the earth have not heard an intelligent presentation of the gospel and that they will not have the opportunity unless someone who knows the Savior crosses the boundaries of their culture, identifies with them, and builds a bridge of love? Can you be that person? One who will answer the cry of the lost multitudes: "Come over and help us!" If you cannot go yourself, can you support one to take your place?

Is your name being called? "Suzie, Ralph—Simon son of John, do you truly love me? Then feed my sheep."

Test of Obedience

Lest some think that ministry is optional, Jesus concludes His discourse with the command: ". . .'Follow me,' " (John 21:19, 22). *Obedience to Christ is finally the test of our love.*

Actually this truth was put to the disciples in the beginning, when they were asked to come with Him (John 1:39, 43). It was their obedience to His word that enabled them to become a part of His fellowship and continue to learn of Him. He did not ask them to follow what they did not know to be true; but what they did understand, He expected them to practice.

" 'Not everyone who says to me, "Lord, Lord," ' " Jesus said, " 'will enter the kingdom of heaven,' " but only those who do the will of God (Matt. 7:21; cf. Luke 6:46). " 'If you love me, you will obey what I command' " (John 14:15). " 'Whoever has my commands and obeys them, he is the one

who loves me' " (John 14:21; cf. 14:23, 24). " 'If you obey
my commands, you will remain in my love, just as I have
obeyed my Father's commands and remain in his love' " (John
15:10; cf. 15:12).

Christ's obedience to the will of the Father who sent Him
was the example of what perfect love means. The giving of
Himself on the cross was the climax of that commitment.
Since that offering had been made in His mind before the
worlds were made (Rev. 13:8; Acts 2:23), each step that He
took on earth was a conscious experience of the love of God.

Taking up the Cross

In the same sense of obedience, there is a cross for all who
would follow in His steps (Matt. 16:24; Mark 8:34; Luke
9:23). Not that any disciple can duplicate His atoning sacrifice, of course. No one could do that work but the perfect
man, and it has been finished once and for all. But the principle of obedience to the mission of God, whatever it entails,
remains as the basis for continuing in the joy of Christ's love.

To be sure, such obedience is costly. It will mean the
surrender of our lives in loving submission to His will (Mark
8:35; 10:21; Matt. 16:25; 19:21; Luke 9:24; 14:33; 18:22).
For Peter it would actually lead to an early martyrdom, as
Jesus told him: " 'When you are old you will stretch out your
hands,' " a way of indicating the manner of his death. Peter
would be led to a place of execution where no man would
want to go (John 21:18). According to tradition, it happened
just that way. He was stretched out on a cross, and crucified
upside down.

The mode of physical death, however, is of no importance.
What matters is the crucifixion of our own self-centeredness,
"so that the body of sin might be rendered powerless" (Rom.

6:6, footnoted translation; cf. Gal. 2:20; 5:24). Herein is the secret of that love which casts out all fear (1 John 4:7–21).

A Personal Decision

" 'Follow me,' " Jesus said to Peter. With this the Master moved on, perhaps going to the mount where other believers were waiting for Him, at which time He would give them the Great Commission to go and disciple all nations (Matt. 28:18–20).

John also started to follow, and noticing him out of the corner of his eye, Simon asked, " 'Lord, what about him?' " (John 21:21). Would John also meet a martyr's death? Or would he, perchance, have it easier?

Jesus turned to Peter and answered, " 'If I want him to remain alive until I return, what is that to you? You must follow me' " (John 21:22). As if to say, what has John's situation got to do with your obedience? Whatever happens to your fellow believers, whether they have more comfortable lots in life, is not your problem. Face up to your own responsibility. "You must follow me."

Isn't that where the issue rests with us all? Finally all of us must answer for ourselves.

Some years ago I was gripped by the account of five missionaries who were killed while seeking to make contact with the Auca Indians in Ecuador. What so arrested my attention was an interview a reporter had with the widowed wives. "Why would God permit this to happen?" he asked. "After all, were not the men on an errand of mercy?"

One of the wives, turning to the incredulous man, quietly replied: "Sir, God delivered my husband from the possibility of disobedience."

"But that is too reckless, too dangerous," you might say.

Yes, it may be. Nevertheless, it is what made the apostolic Christians more than conquerors. Throwing caution to the wind, they lived as those who already reckoned themselves to be dead—dead to sin, dead to the world—but alive unto God.

Would that this kind of obedience to Christ characterized the church today!

I read about a little boy who was told by his doctor that he could save his sister's life by giving her some blood. The six-year-old was near death, and her only chance of recovering was a blood transfusion from someone who had previously conquered the illness. Since the two children had the same rare blood type, the boy was the ideal donor.

"Johnny, would you give your blood for Mary?" the doctor asked.

The boy hesitated. His lower lip started to tremble. Then he smiled, and said, "Sure, Doc, I'll give my blood for my sister."

Soon the two children were wheeled into the operating room—Mary, pale and thin; Johnny, robust and the picture of health. Neither spoke, but when their eyes met, Johnny grinned.

As his blood siphoned into Mary's veins, one could almost see new life come into her tired body. The ordeal was almost over when Johnny's brave little voice broke the silence. "Say, Doc, when do I die?"

It was only then that the doctor realized what that moment of hesitation, that trembling of the lips meant. For little Johnny, in his naïveté, actually thought that in giving his blood to his sister he was giving up his life. And in that brief moment he made his great decision.[4]

---

4. Narrated by Myron L. Morris, M.D., in *Coronet* (November 1948).

He Speaks to You

In a way, that is the kind of decision Jesus asks for in the Great Commission. It is a commitment of love unto death. And once made, it is a decision renewed daily as we follow Him.

As you know the command of your Lord, what is your decision? Do you hear Him call your name? "Bud, Jane— Simon son of John, I am the Lord with all authority in heaven and earth. Do you truly love Me?

"Then disciple My sheep, as I have discipled you.

"And whatever your appointed task in this world, renounce the right to yourself, take up your cross, and as you follow Me, I will be with you always, even to the end of the age."

Study Guide

Preface

God has called us to "go out" with Him—to move with His purpose to make a people who will fill the earth with His glory. From the very first page of the Bible His plan unfolds, finally coming into focus in the life, death, and resurrection of Jesus Christ. He is the Incarnation of the Great Commission. And as He was sent into the world, so now He sends His disciples.

Before us lies the objective. Will we heed the call?

Write It Out

1. God's plan is to raise up _____ .

2. God used Abraham's seed to bring _____ .

3. Solomon prayed that _____ might know and fear the _____ .

4. Jesus anticipated that day when _____ "will . . . take their places . . . in the kingdom of heaven."

5. Before the nations could bow before Him, Jesus would have to reconcile mankind to God through _____ .

6. The coming of the Kingdom awaited the _____ .

7. _____ means "to bear testimony to what is known personally to be true."

8. God's purpose is to _____ .

Check the Scripture

1. List three promises God made to Abraham.

2. Each of the four evangelists sees the Great Commission from a slightly different perspective. List the key point in each Gospel writer's witness.

3. Describe the desired end of Matthew's version of the Great Commission.

Questions for Thought

1. Why do you think so much confusion surrounds the Great Commission? What has been your understanding?

2. How does the objective of the commission emerge in the creation of man and woman? Why does God's purpose in creation assure the completion of His plan to make a people for His glory? Why is its fulfillment delayed?

3. How does God's call of Abraham foreshadow the Great Com-

mission? What is expected, and what is promised? How is the vision of the coming glory kept alive through the Old Testament?

4. Why does everything about the gathering of the nations point to Christ? What does the coming of the Son of Man mean? How did this knowledge affect the life of Jesus? What did its realization require?

5. Why do you surmise that all four of the Gospels include a version of the Great Commission? When are they given? What connection do they have with the resurrection?

6. What is the force of John's account? What is the relationship between the apostolic mission and the Holy Spirit?

7. How does Luke record the commission? What does witnessing imply? Where does the power come from?

8. What does Mark emphasize? How is preaching the gospel understood? Who is a herald?

9. In what sense does Matthew's version incorporate the thrust of the other three accounts, including Christ's affirmation, mandate, and promise?

10. How is the universal scope of the commission stressed in all the Gospels? Why does everything come down to world evangelization? What does it mean?

11. Where do you go when you go "out" with God? What is your destination?

12. Why does the Great Commission call us to measure our lives by the heavenly vision?

Part One
The Affirmation

Evangelism starts with Jesus—who He is and what He has done for us. But even the first-century disciples had doubts until they had seen the risen Lord for themselves.

Jesus came to them and assured them of His conquest of death. They would not go out into the world in their own strength. Rather they would go forth in His power, confident that He is Lord of the universe.

We, too, are to preach a victorious Christ to a hopeless world. Though it be a slow and difficult task, we know that finally every knee shall bow before Him.

Write It Out

1. Jesus has _____ ; His authority reaches across the vast expanse of the planet and unto the farthest star.

2. The redemption of mankind clearly centers in _____ _____ .

3. Christ sets Himself before us, not only as the _____ , but also as the _____ .

4. In the schedule of eternity, the Great Commission is _____ _____ .

Check the Scripture

1. List three biblical incidents that show the confusion in the minds of the disciples after Christ's crucifixion. How was their perplexity overcome?

2. List verses that emphasize the purpose of the cross.

3. List five ways Jesus used His sovereign power while He was among us in the flesh. What did He expect of the disciples in return?

4. When Jesus returns in glory, three things will happen. List them, with appropriate Scripture verses.

5. Name three ways in which Satan responds to evangelism. What Scriptures tell you this?

6. What attitude did the first-century disciples have toward spreading the gospel? List some Scriptures that provide us with answers to the question, "Whom should I evangelize?"

7. What Scripture in the Book of Revelation assures you that the Great Commission is fulfilled?

Questions for Thought

1. Why do you think the Great Commission begins with Christ's affirmation? Would the same reason pertain today? How is the affirmed principle brought out by the Gospel writers?

2. Why do the resurrection and ascension of Christ now make His

death a baffling problem for the world? When did you face this problem?

3. How does Jesus assert His deity? What does it mean to call Him Lord?

4. Why does everything in our salvation turn on the way we believe in Christ? What right does He have to impose His authority over all creation?

5. How does the world look upon His exclusive claims? Why?

6. What will happen to the people who have not heard the gospel? How will they be judged? Why does responsibility for salvation finally rest with every individual?

7. Why does every advance of the gospel entail conflict? Who is Satan and how pervasive is his power?

8. How does the church militant become the church triumphant? What does this say about the priority of world evangelization?

9. What is the Kingdom over which Christ reigns? In what sense is it present now? In what sense is it future?

10. When will the Kingdom come to consummation?

11. Why is the fulfillment of the Great Commission already celebrated in heaven?

12. What does the certainty of Christ's eternal triumph mean to your ministry? How does His authority affect the way you live every day?

Part Two
The Mandate

Obeying the Great Commission is the only path for the Christian. We cannot "opt out" of this life-style. Though we may adapt our methods, we must ever seek to "make disciples of all nations," teaching them in turn to do the same.

As we do this, we seek to follow Jesus, who has shown us the way in which to carry out His own command. His life was a long, powerful example of disciple making. As we turn to Him, we learn to accomplish the task before us.

Write It Out

1. The evangelistic imperative to preach the gospel and to bring persons into baptism aims to _____ .

2. Disciples of Christ _____ , and by the same virtue, they develop in _____ .

3. The Great Commission enunciates the strategy in Jesus' own ministry _____ .

4. A _____ must take place in the human heart, a change so radical that self-indulgent sheep become _____
_____ .

5. In the incarnation, Jesus assumed the _____ .

6. In a deliberate way, Jesus invested His life in _____ .

7. Whether one sowed or reaped, Jesus wanted the disciples to realize _____ .

8. Unless _____ directs the daily life of the whole body, the church cannot function as it should.

9. With those persons who do not yet know the Savior, your relationship becomes _____ .

10. According to their _____ and _____ , all can do something.

11. In _____ we enter most deeply into that love which drove Him into the world.

Check the Scripture

1. Recall some examples of the response of the multitudes to Jesus. Compare this with the response of the religious leaders. Were the multitudes better than their leaders? Why or why not? What can we learn from this?

2. List four verses that tell what Jesus asked of His disciples. Did they always live up to that? What did Jesus see in His disciples?

3. How did Jesus have the disciples assist Him in ministry? De-

scribe the progression that took place, noting Scripture verses
that prove your points.

4. What was Jesus describing in the parable of the vine and the
branches? Which verse in this passage speaks most to you, and
why?

5. Note several implications for the Great Commission that you
learn from the High Priestly Prayer of Jesus in John 17.

Questions for Thought

1. What is the command of the Great Commission? How do the
participles support the controlling verb?

2. What is the difference between a convert and a disciple? Why
is this distinction so crucial in the mandate? How does the
command show the genius of Christ's strategy to reach the
world?

3. How does our Lord's way of life become the interpretation of
His commission? Why must we be careful to distinguish between methods and principles?

4. What about the way Christ chose to live indicates a different
value system from that of the world? How do His birth and
growing up call attention to His choice?

5. Why were people drawn to Jesus? How is the same appeal seen
in your life?

6. What was the problem of the multitudes? How was their condition like that of people today?

7. Why does Jesus concentrate upon making disciples? Where did He find them? What qualified them for attention?

8. How did Jesus develop the disciples' potential? How can the same pattern unfold in your life? What about your shortcomings?

9. What makes the principle of association so powerful in teaching values? How have you seen this in your experience?

10. How does Jesus get people involved in ministry?

11. Once started, how does Jesus keep the disciples going? How are you made accountable?

12. What is meant by fruit bearing? Why is it the key to world evangelization? How does this relate to the priesthood of believers?

13. Where do you begin to make disciples? Who are your natural peers?

14. How do you develop family-style relationships with disciples? In what ways are they getting involved in ministry? How do you check up on them?

15. When will your disciples be able to establish a life-style of the Great Commission? How can you help them project their plans for the future?

16. Why is prayer ultimately the index of your priorities in life? How do your prayers now reflect your vision of the coming Kingdom?

Part Three
The Promise

Without the power of the Holy Spirit, Christians could never succeed at making disciples. He is the Person of God who makes real in our lives what Christ has accomplished for us. Through His indwelling Presence, each believer can minister in the love of Jesus. He is Counselor and Guide, and by His power, we can live every day in fulfillment of the Great Commission.

Write It Out

1. God acts as the Father in _____ ; He is seen as the Son in _____ ; but He moves as the Spirit in _____ .

2. Once we have been _____ , the Spirit continues to _____ growing children of God.

3. From beginning to end, partaking of the _____ is the Spirit's work.

4. Clearly the Spirit was ever present in Christ to _____ .

5. As the Spirit fulfilled God's saving work in Christ, so also He would enable His disciples to _____ , to the ends of the earth.

6. Pentecost marked the beginning of an era that would continue until _____ .

7. Receiving the Spirit in fullness requires that _____ .

Check the Scripture

1. Note some references to the Spirit's work in the Old Testament. What implications does this have for the way God moves in the world?

2. List some of the renewing work the Spirit does in us, providing relevant Scripture texts.

3. How is the work of the Spirit apparent in the life of Christ? What verses stand out in your mind?

4. What difficulties would the disciples face, once Jesus had left them? Observe how the coming of the Spirit speaks to the problem.

5. Read John 14:1—16:33. List every promise of the Spirit in the passage and its results in the disciples' lives.

Questions for Thought

1. Why do you suppose Jesus' promise of the Holy Spirit concludes the Great Commission?

2. How is the Spirit first introduced in the Bible? What does this indicate about the Trinity?

3. Why does every person need to be "born again"? How does it happen?

4. How do you grow in spiritual life? What is the witness of the Holy Spirit?

5. Why would the Spirit be so active in the unfolding history of Israel?

6. What is the Spirit's role in reference to the Word of God? Explain what is meant by the inspiration of the Scripture. Why is this crucial in making disciples?

7. What role does the Spirit have in the birth of Jesus? How does this relate to the deity of Christ?

8. What role does the Spirit have in accomplishing the mission of Christ? Explain the unpardonable sin.

9. How does the Spirit continue Christ's work in His disciples today? In what sense do you see yourself involved in a "greater" work even than Jesus?

10. What does Jesus mean by "another Counselor"? Why would this teaching be so comforting to His disciples?

11. In His ultimate ministry, what is the supreme work of the Holy Spirit? How does this relate to the promise of the Great Commission?

12. What happened at Pentecost to make the disciples powerful witnesses? How is this different from the way the Spirit worked in the Old Testament era? Why was it necessary for Jesus to complete His mission and return to the throne before the Spirit could be poured out in this way?

13. What is the infilling of the Spirit? How is one filled—and kept filled—by the Spirit?

14. Why do people experience the promise of the Spirit in different ways? Describe your own experience.

Epilogue

Once we experience the call and the provision God has made for us, we have not completed the task. Each of us needs to ask, *What will I do about this?* It comes down to what we love. We need to involve our hearts, as well as our heads, in the decision to fulfill the Great Commission.

The Bible provides us with the example of Peter, who had already denied His Lord. Still, Jesus forgave Peter and called him to "follow Me." Despite our failures, we can seek forgiveness and return to service. If we love Him, we will obey His command to disciple all nations.

Write It Out

1. Observe that _____ is the object of love, not a _____ , not a _____ , not a _____ .

2. His mission in the flesh now accomplished, Jesus tells His disciples to _____ .

3. Someone with the heart of Christ must _____ , tell them _____ , and lead them _____ .

4. Christ's obedience to the will of the Father who sent Him was the example of _____ .

Check the Scripture

1. Read John 21:1–23. With which persons do you identify most? What message does God have for you in these verses? How will this influence your vision of the Great Commission?

2. Was it true that Jesus saved others, but could not save Himself from the cross? Why? Provide appropriate Scripture references.

3. What are some of the commands to obedience that Jesus makes? How are these related to the Great Commission?

Questions for Thought

1. What is the Great Commandment? How can it be said that it is the spring from which the Great Commission flows?

2. Why does everything revealed by God ultimately center on Christ? What does this mean for world evangelization?

3. What does Jesus imply when He asks, "Do you love me more than these?" Is there any reason that He would direct this question to you?

4. How is Peter's response like your own? Why does Christ's knowledge of all things affect your love?

5. Why is ministry inseparable from love? How does Jesus make this clear at the cross?

6. Who are the sheep Jesus asks us to tend? Where do you find them? How do they need care? What is your ministry to them?

7. In what sense do the unreached peoples of the earth have a priority upon our concern? How is this seen in your life?

8. What finally is the test of love? Why?

9. How is taking up the cross related to love?

10. Why does it come down to a choice? As you know the Great Commission, what is your decision?